THE BEATLES

THE STORIES BEHIND THE SONGS 1967-1970

Steve Turner

CARLTON
BOOKS

This book is dedicated to the memory of
T-Bone Burnett and Larry Norman in memory
of many hours of Beatle-talk over the years.

THIS IS A CARLTON BOOK

First published by Carlton Books Limited 1994
This edition published by
Carlton Books Limited 2009

Managing Art Director: Lucy Coley
Design: Barbara Zuñiga
Executive editor: Rod Green
Editor: Ian Gittins
Picture research: Paul Langan
Production: Claire Hayward

COPYRIGHT CREDITS

PICTURE CREDITS

CONTENTS

PREFACE

This book tells the stories behind the Beatles' songs, which I've defined as songs written and recorded by the Beatles. It looks at the how, why and where of the songwriting and traces the inspiration back to source.

Having said that, this is not a book about how the Beatles recorded the songs, nor about who played what on which sessions. Mark Lewisohn has done that job definitively in The Complete Beatles Recording Sessions. Neither is it a book of in-depth musical analysis. For this approach, see Twilight Of The Gods by Professor Wilfrid Mellers (Schirmer Books, 1973) or The Songwriting Secrets Of The Beatles by Dominic Pedler (Omnibus Press, 2003).

Also exemplary is Revolution in the Head by Ian MacDonald (Fourth Estate, 1994). MacDonald takes the same song-by-song approach that this book takes and his insights and depth of knowledge about popular music of the sixties are unparalleled.

This is also not a book that explains what the Beatles 'were really trying to say'. Although I've given outlines of many songs and have referred to psychological factors that I believe influenced the standpoint of the writing, I've left the task of interpretation to others. If you do want to know what Paul was saying, read a book like Paul McCartney: From Liverpool To Let It Be by Howard DeWitt (Horizon Books, 1992) or, if you want to catch the drift of John's intellectual development, read The Art and Music of John Lennon by John Robertson (Omnibus, 1990) or John Lennon's Secret by David Stuart Ryan (Kozmik Press, 1982).

What I have tried to do is simply to tell the story of how each song came into being. It could have been a musical inspiration, such as trying to write in the style of Smokey Robinson. It could have been a phrase that just wouldn't go away, like the 'waves of sorrow, pools of joy' line that compelled John to write 'Across The Universe'. Or it could have been an incident like the death of socialite Tara Browne which led to the writing of a section of 'A Day In The Life'.

My primary source has been the words of the Beatles themselves. I was fortunate enough to meet John, interviewing him and Yoko at the Apple office in Savile Row in the summer of 1971, shortly before Imagine was released. I remember complimenting him on the personal nature of his new songs that had come after an intense period of therapy. "My songs have always been personal," he responded. "'Help!'

was personal. 'You've Got To Hide Your Love Away' was personal. 'I'm A Loser' was personal. I've always been on that kick."

I didn't meet Paul until 1992 when I was asked to help Linda in the writing of the text for her photographic book *Linda McCartney's Sixties: Portrait Of An Era*. I had hoped that Paul would contribute his own memories but he decided that he couldn't just dip into a project like this and yet didn't have the time to make a full commitment. He did, however, point out some discrepancies in the stories I had collected so far which I was then able to change.

The most reliable comments on the songs being those made by the Beatles themselves, I've drawn extensively on the published interviews I have personally collected since beginning my first Beatles' scrapbook in 1963. Those that I had missed, I searched out at the National Newspaper Library and the National Sound Archives in London. There were seven invaluable written accounts which I found myself coming back to repeatedly and without which I wouldn't have known where to start. In order of publication these were: Alan Aldridge's interview with Paul McCartney published as *A Good Guru's Guide To The Beatles' Sinister Songbook* in the *Observer* magazine, London, on November 26, 1967; *The Beatles* by Hunter Davies, 1968; *Lennon: The Greatest Natural Songwriter of our Time* by Mike Hennessey in Record Mirror, October 2, 1971 (reprinted in Hit Parade, April 1972); *Lennon Remembers* by Jann Wenner, 1971; *I Me Mine* by George Harrison, 1980, *The Playboy Interviews* with John Lennon and Yoko Ono, 1981 and *Paul McCartney: Many Years From Now* by Barry Miles (1997). There were also two radio series which shed light on the songwriting: Mike Read's *McCartney*

On McCartney, broadcast on BBC Radio 1 during 1989, and *The Lost Lennon Tapes*, an American production featuring demo tapes from John's private collection which Yoko had allowed to be broadcast for the first time.

As informative as all these were, they didn't tell me the whole story. Many of the anecdotes are already well known. I wanted to interview the people who were around when the songs were written, or who had even been the subject of songs. I also wanted to track down the newspaper stories which had provided ideas, the books from which they'd taken lines and the places which had inspired them. I wanted to surprise even the remaining Beatles themselves because I knew that they didn't know who Mr Kite really was or what happened to the girl whose story inspired 'She's Leaving Home'.

The definitive book on this subject won't be written until John's and George's journals, letters and work books are made public and Paul and Ringo sit down in front of a microphone and share everything they remember about the 208 songs which the Beatles recorded. The chances are, though, that John's material will remain locked in vaults for the foreseeable future because much of it refers to people still living and Yoko believes that it is too sensitive to release. The six-part television series *The Beatles Anthology* and the accompanying 'biography' of the Beatles was disappointing to anyone expecting the remaining members of the Beatles to tell hitherto-untold stories.

That's why it was worth compiling this book. It may be the closest we'll ever get to understanding how the Beatles conjured up their songwriting magic.

Steve Turner
London, November 1998 and March 2005

INTRODUCTION

The second half of the Beatles' career saw them pushing the popular song form as far as they could then imagine it going. I can still remember my surprise on first hearing 'Paperback Writer' because the words of the title were so unlike anything I'd heard in a chart song before. Pop songs were about girls and cars and dancing, not about paperback books or prospective authors.

From 1966 onwards the Beatles didn't seem to consider any subject as inappropriate. At least half the songs on *Revolver* were nothing to do with love and their primary inspiration was no longer the work of other artists. They grabbed song ideas from overheard conversations, anecdotes, newspaper headlines, esoteric books, posters, dreams, TV commercials, paintings and everyday occurrences. They were equally voracious musically, listening to Asian music, avant-garde jazz, musique concrete and experimenting with the possibilities of tampering with magnetic tape.

Revolver, Sgt. Pepper's Lonely Hearts Club Band and the soundtracks for *Magical Mystery Tour* and *Yellow Submarine* all developed from the pursuit of altered states of consciousness. *The Beatles* (*The White Album*), although mostly written during a meditation course in India, marked a return to basics – comic book stories, guttural blues, folk style guitar – and a break with their recent psychedelic past. *Let It Be*, another film soundtrack, was an attempted return to the music that had first inspired them. *Abbey Road* reprised their good points while showing that they were still capable of surprise.

This period of their career saw George Harrison emerging as a composer and John playing less of a central role in the Beatles as Yoko Ono loomed larger in his life. In 1964 and 1965 John had been

From 1966 onwards, the Beatles devoutly pursued altered states of consciousness.

a major contributor to the group's hit singles. After *Sgt. Pepper*, Paul came to dominate. 'Hello Goodbye,' 'Magical Mystery Tour,' 'Lady Madonna,' 'Hey Jude', 'Get Back' and 'Let It Be;' were all written by Paul. The partnership that produced 'She Loves You' and 'I Want To Hold Your Hand' was over.

Almost forty years after the band stopped playing together, their songs still mean a lot to us. For those of us who grew up with them they are like old friends that we never tire of meeting. Because they brightened up our lives and perhaps even helped in awakening our intellectual and spiritual curiosity our feelings towards them are forever warm. Finding out where they came from helps us find out where we came from.

SGT PEPPER'S LONELY HEARTS CLUB BAND

The fruitful period which produced the singles 'Penny Lane' and 'Strawberry Fields Forever' as well as the *Sgt Pepper* album was the first in which the Beatles could be totally devoted to the studio because they were free of touring commitments. They took an unprecedented 105 hours to record both sides of the single and then a further five months to complete the album.

Paul conceived the album as a show staged by a fictional Edwardian brass band transported through time into the psychedelic age and played, of course, by the electronically equipped Beatles. Released in June 1967, *Sgt Pepper* was the album of what became known as 'The Summer Of Love' – a brief season when the hippie ethic developed in San Francisco seemed to pervade the whole of the Western world. For anyone who was young at the time, the music automatically evokes the sight of beads and kaftans, the sound of tinkling bells and the aroma of marijuana masked by joss sticks. Despite this, there were only four songs on *Sgt Pepper* – 'Lucy In The Sky With Diamonds', 'She's Leaving Home', 'Within You Without You' and 'A Day In The Life' – that even alluded to the social upheaval caused by the changing youth culture.

The rest of the songs were very British pop songs, tackling a range of domestic subjects from neighbourliness ('A Little Help From My Friends') and self-improvement ('Getting Better'), through suburban living ('Good Morning, Good Morning') and home decoration ('Fixing A Hole'), to Victorian entertainment ('Being For The Benefit Of Mr Kite'). The language of the songs was often deliberately antiquated – 'guaranteed to raise a smile', 'may I inquire discreetly', 'meeting a man from the motor trade', 'a splendid time is guaranteed for all', 'indicate

The audacious *Sgt Pepper's Lonely Hearts Club Band* became synonymous with 1967's remarkable Summer of Love.

precisely what you mean to say' – as if this really was an Edwardian production staged by the good Sergeant Pepper and his men from the local Lonely Hearts club.

Yet, the spirit of 1967 suffused the album in significant ways. It was a fruit of the belief that limits to the imagination were culturally imposed and should therefore be challenged. Anything that seemed technically possible was worth an attempt from a climaxing orchestral frenzy on 'A Day In The Life' to a note of such a high frequency that only a dog could hear it on the play-out groove.

Sgt Pepper was one of the first records to have a gatefold sleeve, printed lyrics, decorated inner bag, free gift and a cover designed by a celebrated artist. Its reputation as the first 'concept album' though is undeserved. Merle Travis's *Folk Songs From the Hills* (1947) was a concept album as was Frank Sinatra's *In The Wee Small Hours* (1955) and, more recently, Johnny Cash's *Blood Sweat and Tears* (1963) and *Bitter Tears* (1965). Indeed, it's arguable whether *Sgt Pepper* was a concept album at all. The only unifying theme was the Pepper song and its reprise and the photographs on the sleeve. There was no theme holding the individual songs together. "Basically *Sgt Pepper* was McCartney's album, not Lennon's," says Barry Miles, who was the group's main contact on the London underground scene at the time. "People make the mistake of thinking it must have been Lennon's because he was so hip. Actually, he was taking so many drugs and trying to get rid of his ego that it was much more McCartney's idea."

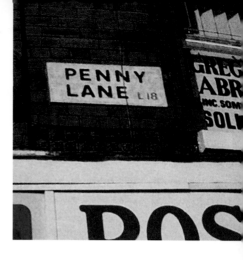

PENNY LANE

Penny Lane is a Liverpool street but also the name given to the area that surrounds its junction with Smithdown Road. None of the places mentioned in 'Penny Lane' exists in the lane itself. Anyone not raised in this area of Liverpool might find it , as musician and art critic George Melly once put it, a "dull suburban shopping centre". But to Paul and John, who had spent their early years in the area, it represented a time in their lives when everyone appeared to be friendly and the sun shone for ever in a clear blue sky. Living in the bubble of fame their memories of childhood were more gilded. As John had observed in 'She Said, She Said', 'When I was a boy, everything was right.'

The band ensured that Penny Lane in Liverpool has become one of Britain's most famous street names.

John had incorporated Penny Lane into an early draft of 'In My Life', but it was Paul who made it work. He created a Liverpool street scene that could have been taken from a children's picture book with a pretty nurse, a jolly barber, an eccentric banker, a patriotic fireman and some friendly passers by. "It's part fact," he admitted. "It's part nostalgia." At first it sounds as though a summer scene is being described ('blue suburban skies') but then rain is mentioned as well as someone selling poppies (November 11). The point is that the song is a series of snapshots, not all of them necessarily taken on the same day.

There was a barber's shop in Penny Lane, run by a Mr Bioletti who claimed to have cut hair for John, Paul and George as children; there were two banks (Barclays and Lloyds), a fire station in Allerton Road and, in the middle of the roundabout, a shelter. The banker without a mac and fireman with a portrait of the Queen in his pocket were Paul's embellishments. "I wrote that the barber had photographs of every head he'd had the pleasure of knowing," said

Paul. "Actually he just had photos of different hairstyles. But all the people who come and go do stop and say hello."

Finger pie was a Liverpudlian sexual reference included in the song to amuse the locals. "It was just a nice little joke for the Liverpool lads who like a bit of smut," said Paul. "For months afterwards, girls serving in local chip shops had to put up with requests for 'fish and finger pie'."

Liverpool poet Roger McGough, who was in the music and satire group Scaffold with Paul's brother Mike, believes that 'Penny Lane' and 'Strawberry Fields' were significant because, for the first time, British rather than American landmarks were being celebrated in rock'n'roll.

"The Beatles were starting to write songs about home," McGough says. "They began to draw on things like the rhymes we used to sing in the streets and old songs our parents remembered from the days of the music halls. Liverpool didn't have a mythology until they created one."

Today, because of the song, Penny Lane is a Liverpool tourist attraction and this itself has altered the area. The original street signs were stolen years ago and their replacements have had to be screwed to walls and placed beyond easy reach. The barber's shop has become a unisex salon with a picture of the Beatles displayed in the window. The shelter on the roundabout has been renovated and re-opened as Sgt Pepper's Bistro. The Penny Lane Wine Bar has the song's lyrics painted above its windows.

PENNY LANE

Written:	Lennon/McCartney
Length:	3' 03"
UK single release:	February 17, 1967 as double A-side with 'Strawberry Fields Forever'
UK chart position:	2
US single release:	February 13, 1967 as double A-side with 'Strawberry Fields Forever'
US chart position:	1

STRAWBERRY FIELDS FOREVER

In the autumn of 1966, John went to Spain to film the role of Private Gripweed in Dick Lester's *How I Won The War*. While relaxing between shots on the beach at Almeira he began composing 'Strawberry Fields Forever', a song he conceived as a slow talking-blues. Further work on the song took place in a large house he was renting in nearby Santa Isabel.

The song began with what would become the second verse in the recorded version. It was a meditation on the conviction he'd had since he was a child that he was somehow different from everyone else; that he saw and felt things that other people didn't. In the earliest preserved version of his Spanish tapes he starts, "No one is on my wavelength", later changing the line to "No one I think is in my tree", presumably to disguise what could be seen as arrogance. He was saying that he believed that no one could tune in to his way of thinking, and that therefore he must either be a genius ('high') or insane ('low'). "I seem to see things in a different way from most people," he once said. It was only on take four of the songwriting tape that he introduced Strawberry Fields (but without the 'forever') and on take five he added the line 'nothing to get mad about' that was later altered to 'nothing to get hung about'. He was already using the deliberately hesitant mode – "er", "that is", "I mean", "I think" – to underline the truth that this was an attempt to articulate concepts that can't actually be put into words.

On his return to England he worked on the song at Kenwood where the final verse was added. It wasn't until he went into the studio that he finished the song by adding the opening verse, a fact that helps to explain why the sentiment of the introduction seems out of joint with the rest of the song.

STRAWBERRY FIELDS FOREVER
Written:
Lennon/McCartney
Length: 4' 10"
UK single release:
February 17, 1967
as double A-side
with 'Penny Lane'
UK chart position: 2
US single release:
February 13, 1967
as double A-side
with 'Penny Lane'
US chart position: 8*
Although 'Penny Lane'/'Strawberry Fields Forever was a double A-side single, US chart compilers calculated the two songs' sales separately

In the completed version a place is made to represent a state of mind. Strawberry Fields (John added the 's') was a Salvation Army orphanage in Beaconsfield Road, Woolton, a five-minute walk from his home in Menlove Avenue. A huge Victorian building set in wooded grounds, it was a place where John would go with his Aunt Mimi for summer fêtes but also somewhere that he would sneak into during evenings and at weekends with friends such as Pete Shotton and Ivan Vaughan. It became their private adventure playground.

These illicit visits were, to John, like Alice's escapades down the rabbit hole and through the looking glass. He felt that he was entering another world, a world that more closely corresponded with his inner world, and as an adult he would associate these moments of bliss with his lost childhood and also with a feeling of drug-free psychedelia.

In his *Playboy* interview of 1980 he told David Sheff that he would 'trance out into alpha' as a child, seeing 'hallucinatory images' of his face when looking into a mirror. He said it was only when he later discovered the work of artists like the surrealists that he realised that he wasn't mad but a part of 'an exclusive club that sees the world in those terms'.

13

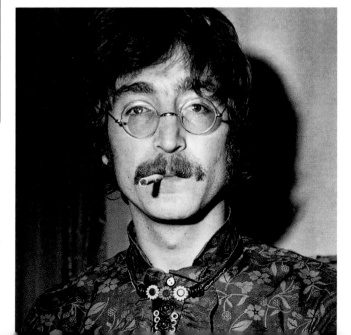

'Strawberry Fields Forever' was named after a Salvation Army orphanage in Woolton, a five-minute walk from John's home in Menlove Avenue.

SGT PEPPER'S LONELY HEARTS CLUB BAND

Success meant that the public expected the Beatles not only to deliver another artistic masterpiece but a prophetic vision. To relieve this pressure, Paul developed the personae of Sgt Pepper and his musicians, an identity that would give the band more creative freedom. They had become self-conscious as the Beatles but as the Lonely Hearts Club Band they would have nothing to live up to.

Paul conceived the idea on a flight back to London from Nairobi on November 19th 1966. During an earlier part of this holiday when he was in France he had used a facial disguise in order to travel incognito. This had led him to consider how free the Beatles would be if they could adopt a group disguise.

The conceit, however, wasn't sustained beyond the opening track and the reprise although it succeeded in giving the impression to many people that *Sgt Pepper's Lonely Hearts Club Band* was a 'concept album'. "The songs, if you listen to them, have no connection at all," George Martin admits. "Paul said, 'Why don't we make the band 'Pepper' and Ringo 'Billy Shears' because it gives a nice beginning to the thing? It wasn't really a concept album at all. It was just a question of me trying to make something coherent by doing segues as much as possible." Later on, Martin came up with the idea for the reprise, which helped to wrap it all up.

Sgt Pepper and his band achieved the feat of being very West Coast 1967 (you could picture their name on a psychedelic poster for the Avalon Ballroom in San Francisco) at the same time as remaining quintessentially English (you could imagine them playing on an Edwardian summer lawn). Paul had intended to play it both ways, writing old-fashioned lyrics delivered with a satirical psychedelic

SGT PEPPER'S LONELY HEARTS CLUB BAND
Written:
Lennon/
McCartney
Length: 2' 02"
UK release:
Sgt Pepper's Lonely Hearts Club Band album, June 1, 1967
US release:
Sgt Pepper's Lonely Hearts Club Band album, June 2, 1967

intensity, and using a title that appealed to the late Sixties vogue for long and surreal band names – Jefferson Airplane, Quicksilver Messenger Service, Incredible String Band, Big Brother and the Holding Company. "They're a bit of a brass band in a way," Paul said at the time, "but they're also a rock band because they've got that San Francisco thing."

Sgt Pepper's Lonely Hearts Club Band was both evocative of the West Coast 1967 sound of America and quintessentially English.

The origin of the name Sgt Pepper is disputed. The Beatles' former road manager Mal Evans is sometimes cited as having created it as a jokey substitute for 'salt 'n' pepper'. Others suggest that the name was derived from the popular American soft drink 'Dr Pepper'.

15

WITH A LITTLE HELP
FROM MY FRIENDS

Journalist Hunter Davies was granted a unique insight into the
Beatles' writing methods while working on their eponymous 1968
authorised biography. On the afternoon of March 29, 1967, Davies
went to Paul's house in Cavendish Avenue and watched as Paul and
John worked on 'With A Little Help From My Friends'. It was one of
the first times a journalist had witnessed Lennon and McCartney
composing. "They wanted to do a Ringo-type song," remembers
Davies. "They knew it would have to be for the kids, a sing-along
type of song. That was what they thought was missing on the album
so far. I recorded them trying to get all the rhymes right and
somewhere I've got a list of all the ones they didn't use."

At the beginning of the afternoon, all the writers had was a
chorus line and a bit of a melody. For the first two hours, they
thrashed away on guitars, neither of them getting very far. It was John
who eventually suggested starting each verse with a question. The

---

WITH A LITTLE HELP FROM MY FRIENDS

Written:	Lennon/McCartney
Length:	2' 44"
UK release:	*Sgt Pepper's Lonely Hearts Club Band* album, June 1, 1967
US release:	*Sgt Pepper's Lonely Hearts Club Band* album, June 2, 1967

'With A Little Help From My Friends' began to take shape when John suggested beginning each verse with a question.

17

line, 'Do you believe in love at first sight?' didn't have the right number of syllables and so it became 'a love at first sight'. John answer to this was 'Yes, I'm certain that it happens all the time'. This was then followed by 'Are you afraid when you turn out the light?' but rephrased to 'What do you see when...'.

Cynthia Lennon then came in and suggested 'I'm just fine' as an answer, but John dismissed it saying that 'just' was either a filler or a meaningless word. Instead, he tried 'I know it's mine', eventually coming up with the more substantial 'I can't tell you, but I know it's mine'.

After a few hours of playing around with words, their minds began to wander. They began fooling around, singing 'Can't Buy Me Love' and playing 'Tequila' (a 1958 hit for the Champs) on the piano. "When they got stuck, they would go back and do a rock'n'roll song," remembers Davies. "Sometimes they would sing an Englebert Humperdinck song and just bugger around and then get back to the job in hand."

A recording session was due to begin at seven o'clock and they called Ringo to tell him that his song was ready, even though the lyrics weren't quite there yet. The lyrics were completed in the studio, where ten takes of the song were recorded that night. As John had an injured finger at the time it was initially known as 'Bad Finger Boogie' but was later changed to the rather apt 'With A Little Help From My Friends'.

LUCY IN THE SKY WITH DIAMONDS

One afternoon early in 1967, Julian Lennon came home from his nursery school with a coloured drawing that he said was of his classmate, four-year-old Lucy O'Donnell. Explaining his artwork to his father, Julian said it was Lucy – 'in the sky with diamonds'.

Julian Lennon told his dad that this drawing of a school classmate depicted "Lucy – in the sky with diamonds".

This phrase struck John and triggered off the associations that led to the writing of the dream-like 'Lucy In The Sky With Diamonds', one of three tracks on the *Sgt Pepper* album that were supposed to be 'about drugs'. Although it's unlikely that John would have written such a piece of reverie without ever having experimented with hallucinogenics, this song was equally affected by his love of surrealism, word play and the works of Lewis Carroll.

That the song was a description of an LSD trip seemed to be proved when it was noted that the initials in the title spelt LSD. Yet John consistently denied this both in public and in private, although he was never hesitant to discuss songs that did refer to drugs. He insisted that the title was taken from what Julian had said about his painting. Julian himself recalls, "I don't know why I called it that or why it stood out from all my other drawings but I obviously had an affection for Lucy at that age. I used to show dad everything I'd built or painted at school and this one sparked off the idea for a song about Lucy in the sky with diamonds."

Lucy O'Donnell (who now works as a teacher with special needs' children) lived near the Lennon family in Weybridge and she and Julian were pupils at Heath House, a nursery school run by two old ladies in a rambling Edwardian house. "I can remember Julian at school," says Lucy, who didn't discover that she'd been immortalized in a Beatles' song until she was 13. "I can remember him very well. I can see his face clearly...

LUCY IN THE SKY WITH DIAMONDS

Written:
Lennon/
McCartney

Length: 3' 28"

UK release:
Sgt Pepper's Lonely Hearts Club Band album, June 1, 1967

US release:
Sgt Pepper's Lonely Hearts Club Band album, June 2, 1967

we used to sit alongside each other at proper old-fashioned desks. The house was enormous and they had heavy curtains to divide the classrooms. Julian and I were a couple of little menaces from what I've been told."

John claimed that the hallucinatory images in the song were inspired by the 'Wool And Water' chapter in Lewis Carroll's *Through The Looking Glass*, where Alice is taken down a river in a rowing boat by the Queen, who has suddenly changed into a sheep.

As a child, *Alice's Adventures In Wonderland* and *Through The Looking Glass* were two of John's favourite books. They'd been given to him as birthday presents and in a 1965 interview he claimed that he read both books once a year. In a later interview he claimed that it was partly through reading them that he realized the images in his own mind weren't indications of insanity. "Surrealism to me is reality," he said. "Psychedelic vision is reality to me and always was."

For similar reasons, John was attracted to *The Goon Show*, the British radio comedy show featuring Spike Milligan, Harry Secombe and Peter Sellers which was broadcast by the BBC between June 1952 and January 1960. *The Goon Show* scripts, principally written by Milligan, lampooned establishment figures, attacked post-war stuffiness and popularized surreal humour. The celebrated Beatle 'wackiness' owed a lot to the Goons, as did John's poetry and writing. He told Spike Milligan that 'Lucy In The Sky With Diamonds' and several other songs had been partly inspired by his love of Goon Show dialogue.

"We used to talk about 'plasticine ties' in *The Goon Show* and this crept up in Lucy as 'plasticine porters with looking glass ties'," says Milligan who, as a friend of George Martin, sat in on some of the *Sgt Pepper* sessions. "I knew Lennon quite well. He used to talk a lot about comedy. He was a *Goon Show* freak. It all stopped when he married Yoko Ono. Everything stopped. He never asked for me again."

When Paul arrived at Weybridge to work on the song John had only completed the first verse and the chorus. For the rest of the writing they traded lines and images; Paul coming up with 'newspaper taxis' and 'cellophane flowers', John with 'kaleidoscope eyes'.

19

GETTING BETTER

Much of *Sgt Pepper* was written as the album was being recorded, with John and Paul grabbing inspiration from whatever was happening around them. Hunter Davies was with Paul on one such occasion – when he was struck by the phrase which became the basis of 'Getting Better'. "I was walking around Primrose Hill with Paul and his dog Martha," he says. "It was bright and sunny – the first spring-like morning we'd had that year. Thinking about the weather Paul said, 'It's getting better'. He was meaning that spring was here but he started laughing and, when I asked him why, he told me that it reminded him of something."

The phrase took Paul's mind back to drummer Jimmy Nicol, who briefly became a Beatle in June 1964, substituting on tour for a sick Ringo. Nicol was an experienced musician who had worked with the Spotnicks and Georgie Fame's Blue Flames, but he had to learn to be a Beatle overnight. Called in by George Martin on June 3, he met John, Paul and George that afternoon and was on stage with them in Copenhagen the following night. A week later in Adelaide, after playing just five dates, Nicol was given his fee, together with a jokey 'retirement present', a gold watch. "After every concert, John and Paul would go up to Jimmy Nicol and ask him how he was getting on," says Hunter Davies. "All that Jimmy would ever say was, 'It's getting better'. That was the only comment they could get out of him. It ended up becoming a joke phrase and whenever the boys thought of Jimmy they'd think of 'it's getting better'."

After the walk on Primrose Hill, Paul drove back to his home in St John's Wood and sang the phrase over and over, while picking out a tune on his guitar. Then he worked it out on the piano in his music

GETTING BETTER

Written:
Lennon/
McCartney

Length: 2' 47"

UK release:
Sgt Pepper's Lonely Hearts Club Band
album, June 1, 1967

US release:
Sgt Pepper's Lonely Hearts Club Band
album, June 2, 1967

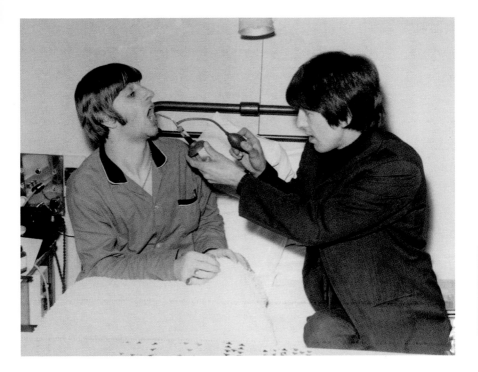

'Getting Better' was inspired by a comment made by replacement Beatles drummer Jimmy Nicol, who filled in in 1964 when Ringo was ill with tonsillitis.

room which had a strange tone that sounded almost out of tune. "That evening John came round," remembers Davies. "Paul suggested writing a song called 'It's Getting Better'. Now and again, they'd write whole songs individually, but mostly one of them had half a song and the other one would finish it off. That's how it was with this one. Paul played what he'd come up with to John and together they finished it."

'Getting Better' proved an interesting example of how they curbed each other's excesses when they worked together. The optimism of Paul's chorus, where everything is improving because of love, is counterbalanced by John's confession that he was once a schoolboy rebel, an angry young man and a wife beater. When Paul sings that things are getting better all the time, John chimes in with 'it couldn't get much worse'.

Asked about the song years later, John admitted it referred to his aggressive tendencies, "I sincerely believe in love and peace. I am a violent man who has learned not to be violent and regrets his violence."

FIXING A HOLE

'Fixing A Hole' was another Sgt Pepper song assumed to refer to drugs. People assumed that Paul was talking about 'fixing' with heroin. But the song really was about renovating his life, allowing himself the freedom to close up the cracks and holes that allowed the enemies of his imagination to leak in. "It's the hole in your make up which lets the rain in and stops your mind from going where it will," as he put it.

Although it wasn't about DIY, Paul may have drawn the images from his Scottish hideaway, High Park, that he had bought in June 1966 on the advice of his accountants. The house, which had 400 acres of grazing land, hadn't been lived in for five years and was in poor condition from the regular battering of rain and sea winds. The brown walls were dark with damp, the only furniture consisted of potato boxes and there was no bath.

Paul decorated this property 'in a colourful way' as remembered by Alistair Taylor, Brian Epstein's assistant who accompanied Paul and Jane on their first visit to High Park. "The brown paint made the farmhouse look like the inside of an Aero bar," he wrote in his book *Yesterday: My Life With The Beatles*. "Paul decided he'd had enough of it so he went into Campbeltown and bought lots of packets of coloured pens. The three of us spent the next few hours just doodling in all these colours, spreading them all over the wall and trying to relieve the gloom."

In 1967, in an interview with artist Alan Aldridge, Paul was probed on the drug associations: "If you're a junky sitting in a room and fixing a hole then that's what it will mean to you, but when I wrote it I meant if there's a crack, or the room is uncolourful, then I'll paint it."

Paul is thought to have drawn the lyrical imagery of 'Fixing A Hole' from High Park, his Scottish bolthole.

FIXING A HOLE
Written:
Lennon/
McCartney
Length: 2' 36"
UK release:
Sgt Pepper's Lonely Hearts Club Band album, June 1, 1967
US release:
Sgt Pepper's Lonely Hearts Club Band album, June 2, 1967

SHE'S LEAVING HOME

In February 1967, Paul came across a newspaper article about a 17-year-old London schoolgirl studying for her A GCE level exams who'd been missing from home for over a week. Her distressed father was quoted as saying, "I cannot imagine why she should run away. She has everything here."

The subject of teenage runaways was topical in 1967. As part of the creation of an alternative society, counter-culture guru Timothy Leary had urged his followers to 'drop out', to abandon education and 'straight' employment. As a result, streams of young people headed for San Francisco, centre of Flower Power. The FBI announced 90,000 runaways that year – a record.

With only the newspaper story to go on, Paul created a moving song about a young girl sneaking away from her claustrophobically respectable home in search of fun and romance in the swinging Sixties. What he didn't know at the time was how accurate his speculation was. He also had no idea that he had met the girl in question just three years before.

The runaway in the story was Melanie Coe, the daughter of John and Elsie Coe, who lived in Stamford Hill, north London. The only differences between her story and the story told in the song are that she met a man from a gambling casino rather than from 'the motor trade', and that she walked out in the afternoon while her parents were at work, rather than in the morning while they were asleep. "The amazing thing about the song was how much it got right about my life," says Melanie. "It quoted the parents as saying 'we gave her everything money could buy,' which was true in my case. I had two diamond rings, a mink coat, hand-made clothes in silk and cashmere and even my own car.

SHE'S LEAVING HOME
Written:
Lennon/
McCartney
Length: 3' 35''
UK release:
Sgt Pepper's Lonely Hearts Club Band
album, June 1, 1967
US release:
Sgt Pepper's Lonely Hearts Club Band
album, June 2, 1967

"Then there was the line 'after living alone for so many years', which really struck home to me because I was an only child and I always felt alone," Melanie continues. "I never communicated with either of my parents. It was a constant battle. I left because I couldn't face them any longer. I heard the song when it came out and thought it was about someone like me but never dreamed it was actually about me. I can remember thinking that I didn't run off with a man from the motor trade, so it couldn't have been me! I must have been in my twenties when my mother said she'd seen Paul on television and he'd said that the song was based on a story in a newspaper. That's when I started telling my friends it was about me."

Melanie's case was a textbook example of the generational friction of the late sixties. Melanie wanted a freedom she'd heard about but could not find at home. Her father was a successful executive and her mother a hairdresser, but their marriage was dry and brittle. They had no religion: to them the most important things in life were respectability, cleanliness and money. "My mother didn't like any of my friends," says Melanie. "I wasn't allowed to bring anyone home. She didn't like me going out. I wanted to act but she wouldn't let me go to drama school. She wanted me to become a dentist. She didn't like the way I dressed. She didn't want me to do anything that I wanted to do. My father was weak. He just went along with whatever my mother said, even when he disagreed with her."

Melanie Carr, seen above behind the Beatles at *Ready Steady Go!* in 1963, became the teenage runaway subject of 'She's Leaving Home'.

It was through music that Melanie found consolation. At the age of 13, she began clubbing in the West End of London and, when the legendary live television show *Ready Steady Go!* started in late 1963, she became a regular dancer on the show. Her parents would often scour the clubs and drag her back home. If she came back late, she would be hit. "When I went out, I could be me," she said. "In fact, in the clubs I was encouraged to be myself and to have a good time. Dancing was my passion. I was crazy for the music of the time and couldn't wait until the next single came out. When the song says 'Something was denied', that something was me. I wasn't allowed to be *me*. I was looking for excitement and affection. My mother wasn't affectionate at all. She never kissed me."

On Friday October 4, 1963, Melanie won a *Ready Steady Go!* mime competition. By coincidence, it happened to be the first time the Beatles were on the show and she was presented with her award by Paul McCartney. Each of the Beatles then gave her a signed message. "I spent that day in the studios going through rehearsals," she says, "so I was around the Beatles most of that time. Paul wasn't particularly chatty and John seemed distant but I did spend time talking to George and Ringo."

Melanie's flight from home took her into the arms of David, a croupier she had met in a club. They rented a flat in Sussex Gardens near Paddington Station and, while out walking one afternoon, they saw her photo on the front page of an evening newspaper. "I immediately went back to the flat and put on dark glasses and a hat," she said. "From then on, I lived in terror that they'd find me. They did discover me after about ten days, because I think I'd let it slip where my boyfriend worked. They talked to his boss who persuaded me to call them up. When they eventually called to see me, they bundled me into the back of their car and drove me home."

To escape from her parents, Melanie married at 18. The marriage didn't last much more than a year and by the age of 21 she had moved to America to live in an ashram and tried to make it as an actress. Melanie now lives in Spain with two children and a partner, buying and selling Fifties Hollywood jewellery. "If I had my life to live over again, I wouldn't choose to do it the same way," Melanie remarks. "What I did was very dangerous but I was lucky. I suppose it is nice to be immortalised in a song but it would have been nicer if it had been for doing something other than running away from home."

BEING FOR THE BENEFIT
OF MR KITE!

In January 1967, the Beatles went to Knole Park near Sevenoaks in Kent to make a promotional film for 'Strawberry Fields Forever'. "There was an antiques shop close to the hotel we were using," says former Apple employee Tony Bramwell. "John and I wandered in and John spotted this framed Victorian circus poster and bought it."

Printed in 1843, the poster proudly announced that Pablo Fanque's Circus Royal would be presenting the 'grandest night of the season' at Town Meadows, Rochdale, Lancashire. The production was to be 'for the benefit of Mr Kite' and would feature 'Mr J. Henderson the celebrated somerset (sic) thrower' who would 'introduce his extraordinary trampoline leaps and somersets over men and horses, through hoops, over garters and lastly through a hogshead of real fire. In this branch of the profession Mr H challenges the world'. Messrs Kite and Henderson were said to assure the public that 'this night's production will be one of the most splendid ever produced in this town, having been some days in preparation'.

John began to write a song using the poster's words. It now hung in his music room and Pete Shotton saw him squinting at the words while he picked out a tune on his piano. John changed a few facts to fit the song. On the poster, Mr Henderson offered to challenge the world, not Mr Kite: the Hendersons weren't 'late of Pablo Fanque's Fair', Kite was 'late of Wells's Circus'. In order to rhyme with 'don't be late', John moved events from Rochdale to Bishopsgate and to rhyme with 'will all be there' he changed the circus to a fair. The original horse was named Zanthus rather than Henry.

Pablo Fanque, Mr Kite and the Hendersons were never more than colourful names to John but records show that, 150 years ago,

**BEING FOR THE
BENEFIT OF
MR KITE!**
Written:
Lennon/
McCartney
Length: 2' 37"
UK release:
*Sgt Pepper's Lonely
Hearts Club Band*
album, June 1,
1967
US release:
*Sgt Pepper's Lonely
Hearts Club Band*
album, June 2,
1967

they were stars in the circus world. Mr Kite was William Kite, son of a circus proprietor, James Kite, and an all-round performer. In 1810 he formed Kite's Pavilion Circus and 30 years later he was with Wells's Circus. He is believed to have worked in Pablo Fanque's Circus from 1843 to 1845.

Pablo Fanque was a multi-talented performer, who became the first black circus proprietor in Britain. His real name was William Darby and he was born in Norwich in 1796 to John and Mary Darby. He started calling himself Pablo Fanque in the 1830s.

The Hendersons were John (wire-walker, equestrian, trampolinist and clown) and his wife Agnes, who was the daughter of circus owner Henry Hengler. The Hendersons travelled all over Europe and Russia during the 1840s and 1850s. The 'somersets' which Mr Henderson performed on 'solid ground' were somersaults, 'garters' were banners held between two people and a 'trampoline' in those days was a wooden springboard rather than stretched canvas.

At the time, John saw 'Being For The Benefit Of Mr Kite!' as a throwaway, telling Hunter Davies, "I was just going through the motions because we needed a new song for *Sgt Pepper* at that moment." By 1980, he had radically revised his opinion. He told *Playboy* interviewer David Sheff: "It's so cosmically beautiful... The song is pure, like a painting, a pure watercolour."

John standing beside the Victorian poster which provided almost all of the names and phrases that were used in 'Being For The Benefit of Mr Kite!'

WITHIN YOU WITHOUT YOU

George became interested in Eastern thought as a consequence of discovering the sitar in 1965 and, having studied the instrument under Ravi Shankar, made his first explicit statement of his new-found philosophy in 'Within You Without You'.

Written as a recollected conversation, the song put forward the view that Western individualism – the idea that we each have our own ego – is based on an illusion that encourages separation and division. In order for us to draw closer and get rid of the 'space between us all', we need to give up this illusion of ego and realize that we are essentially 'all one'. Although the view expressed in 'Within You Without You' was drawn from Hindu teaching, it touched a chord among those experimenting with acid at the time. Through a chemically-induced destruction of ego, acid trippers often felt as if they had been absorbed into a greater 'cosmic consciousness'. The line about gaining the world but losing your soul is taken from a warning given by Jesus and recorded in two of the gospels (Matthew 16, v 26, Mark 8, v 36).

George began to compose the song one night after a dinner party at the home of Klaus Voormann, a German artist and musician he had first met in Hamburg and who had designed the cover for *Revolver*. Voormann was now living in London, married to former *Coronation Street* actress Christine Hargreaves and playing bass for Manfred Mann. Also present at the party were Tony King and Pattie Harrison. King had known the Beatles since they first arrived in London in 1963 and he would later work for Apple in London. "Klaus had this pedal harmonium and George went into an adjoining room and started fiddling around on it," remembers King. "It made

WITHIN YOU WITHOUT YOU
Written:
Harrison
Length: 5' 05"
UK release:
Sgt Pepper's Lonely Hearts Club Band album, June 1, 1967
US release:
Sgt Pepper's Lonely Hearts Club Band album, June 2, 1967

'Within You Without You' was the first time that George put into song the teachings of mentor Ravi Shankar.

these terrible groaning noises and, by the end of the evening, he'd worked something out and was starting to sing snatches of it to us. It's interesting that the eventual recording of 'Within You Without You' had the same sort of groaning sound that I'd heard on the harmonium because John once told me that the instrument you compose a song on determines the tone of a song. A number originally written on the piano sounds totally different to one worked out on a guitar."

King's recollection of the evening is of a typical hip Sixties affair with joints being smoked and lots of cosmic ideas floating around: "We were all on about the wall of illusion and the love that flowed between us but none of us knew what we were talking about. We all developed these groovy voices. It was a bit ridiculous really. It was as if we were sages all of a sudden. We all felt as if we had glimpsed the meaning of the universe.

"When I first met George in 1963, he was Mr Fun, Mr Stay Out All Night," King continues. "Then all of a sudden, he found LSD and Indian religion and he became very serious. Things went from rather jolly weekends, where we'd have steak and kidney pie and sit around giggling, to these rather serious weekends where everyone walked around blissed out and talked about the meaning of the universe. It was never really my cup of tea but we all got caught up in it because we were young, easily influenced, and around famous people. I

"These vibrations that you get through yoga, cosmic chants and things like that are such a buzz," said George, in typically karmic mode.

remember when the Dutch artists Simon and Marijke, who later painted the Apple shop front, were at George's, I got fed up with it all and went down the pub. Just as I was walking down George's drive, Simon and Marijke floated past in yards of chiffon and said in their groovy voices, 'Ooh. Where are you going, man?' I told them I was going for a Guinness. They said,. 'Oh. Say something beautiful for me, will you?'"

In an interview with *International Times* in 1967, George said: "We're all one. The realization of human love reciprocated is such a gas. It's a good vibration which makes you feel good. These vibrations that you get through yoga, cosmic chants and things like that, I mean it's such a buzz. It buzzes you out of everywhere. It's nothing to do with pills. It's just in your own head, the realization. It's such a buzz. It buzzes you right into the astral plane."

None of the other Beatles were present when 'Within You Without You' was recorded. George and Neil Aspinall played tambouras while session musicians played an assortment of instruments including dilruba, tabla, violin and cello. "The Indian musicians on the session weren't hard to organize," remembers George Martin. "What was difficult, though, was writing a score for the cellos and violins that the English players would be able to play like the Indians. The dilruba player, for example, was doing all kinds of swoops and so I actually had to score that for strings and instruct the players to follow.

"The laugh at the very end of the track was George Harrison. He just thought it would be a good idea to out on it," recalls Martin.

WHEN I'M SIXTY-FOUR

Paul has said that the melody to 'When I'm Sixty-Four' was composed on the piano at Forthlin Road, Liverpool, "when I was about 15". This places it in either 1957 or 1958, shortly after he joined John in the Quarry Men. By 1960, Paul was playing a version of it at gigs when the amplification broke down. At the time, he thought of it as "a cabaret tune", written out of respect for the music of the Twenties and Thirties, which his father had played as a young man.

In the midst of psychedelia, the fashions of Jim McCartney's younger days were being revived and it made sense for Paul to dust off his teenage song. Twenties pastiche 'Winchester Cathedral' had been a UK hit for The New Vaudeville Band in September 1966, and *Bonnie and Clyde*, the movie that started a craze for Thirties clothing, was released in 1967.

Although the song was written with his father in mind, it was coincidental that he was 64 when it was eventually released. "My dad

---

WHEN I'M SIXTY-FOUR

Written:	Lennon/McCartney
Length:	2' 37"
UK release:	*Sgt Pepper's Lonely Hearts Club Band* album, June 1, 1967
US release:	*Sgt Pepper's Lonely Hearts Club Band* album, June 2, 1967

was probably only 56 when I wrote it," Paul said, "Retirement age in Britain is 65, so maybe I thought 64 was a good prelude. But probably 64 just worked well as a number."

The song is written as a letter from a socially inept young man who seems to be trying to coax a female he hardly knows into promising him long-term devotion. The official tone of the letter ('drop me a line, stating point of view') paints a convincing picture of this formal young gent who wants to get it all in writing before he signs on the dotted line.

"It was a kind of pastiche," says George Martin. "It was a send-up of the old stuff. The words are slightly mocking. It was also something of his father's music coming out because his father had been a musician in the Twenties. Paul always had that sneaking respect for the old rooty-tooty music."

John claimed that he wouldn't have dreamt of writing anything like 'When I'm Sixty-Four'. "John sneered at a lot of things," says Martin. "But that was part of the collaborative style. They tended to be rivals. They were never Rodgers and Hart. They were more like Gilbert and Sullivan. One would do one thing and the other would say, yeah, I can do better than that and go and do better than that. At the same time, he was thinking – that was bloody good. I wish I could do it."

Paul originally wrote 'When I'm Sixty-Four' when he was 15 and made it an affectionate tribute to his father.

LOVELY RITA

An American friend was visiting Paul and, noticing a female traffic warden, a relatively new British phenomenon, commented: "I see you've got meter maids over here these days." Paul was taken with this alliterative term and began experimenting with it on the piano at his father's home. "I thought it was great," he said. "It got to be 'Rita meter maid' and then 'lovely Rita meter maid'. I was thinking it should be a hate song...but then I thought it would be better to love her." Out of this came the idea for a song about a shy office worker who, having been issued with a parking ticket, seduces the warden in an attempt to get let off the fine. "I was imagining the kind of person I would be to fall for a meter maid," Paul remarked.

Some years later, a traffic warden by the name of Meta Davies, who operated in the St John's Wood area of London, claimed she had inspired the song. Not that she had been seduced by a Beatle but, in 1967, she had booked a certain P McCartney who had, apparently, asked about her unusual name. "His car was parked on a meter where the time had expired," says Meta, "I had to make out a ticket which, at the time, carried a ten shilling fine. I'd just put it on the windscreen when Paul came along and took it off. He looked at it and read my signature that was in full, because there was another M Davies on the same unit. As he was walking away, he turned to me and said, 'Oh, is your name really Meta?' I told him that it was. We chatted for a few minutes and he said, 'That would be a good name for a song. Would you mind if I use it?' And that was that. Off he went."

It may be that Paul had already written 'Lovely Rita' and was flattering her a little, although Meta herself was 22 years his senior and the mother of a teenage daughter. "I was never a Beatles' fan," admits Meta. "But you couldn't help hearing their music. My own daughter used to wait outside the Abbey Road Studios to see them."

LOVELY RITA
Written:
Lennon/
McCartney
Length: 2' 42"
UK release:
*Sgt Pepper's Lonely
Hearts Club Band*
album, June 1,
1967

US release:
*Sgt Pepper's Lonely
Hearts Club Band*
album, June 2,
1967

33

GOOD MORNING
GOOD MORNING

Paul dominated *Sgt Pepper* because John had become a lazy Beatle. He rarely ventured far from home, paid little attention to business and was drawing inspiration, not from contemporary art but from the stuff of domestic life – newspapers, school runs, daytime TV.

'Good Morning, Good Morning' was an accurate summary of his situation and an admission that he had run out of things to say. It was a song about his life of indolence – the result of too many drugs, a cold marriage and days measured out in meals, sleep and television programmes such as *Meet The Wife*. "When he was at home, he spent a lot of his time lying in bed with a notepad," remembers Cynthia of this period. "When he got up he'd sit at the piano or he'd go from one room to the other listening to music, gawping at television and reading newspapers. He was basically dropping out from everything that was happening. He was thinking about things. Everything he was involved in outside the home was pretty high-powered."

While sitting around in this state of mind, odd sounds and scraps of conversation would trigger ideas. It was a television commercial for Kellogg's Corn Flakes that gave John the title and chorus of 'Good Morning, Good Morning'. The black and white commercial featured nothing more than corn flakes being tipped into a bowl. The four-line jingle went: 'Good morning, good morning, The best to you each morning, Sunshine breakfast, Kellogg's Corn Flakes, Crisp and full of fun'.

The 'walk by the old school' was a reference to taking Julian to Heath House and it's likely that the person he hoped would 'turn up at a show' was Yoko Ono who he had met in November 1966. The 'show' would therefore have been an art show, not a theatre performance.

GOOD MORNING, GOOD MORNING

Written:
Lennon/
McCartney

Length: 2'41"

UK release:
Sgt Pepper's Lonely Hearts Club Band album, June 1, 1967

US release:
Sgt Pepper's Lonely Hearts Club Band album, June 2, 1967

A DAY IN THE LIFE

For 'She Said She Said', John had combined two unfinished songs but here, for the first time, he put together an unfinished song of his own with one of Paul's to build the most ambitious track on the album.

John's song was prompted by his interminable newspaper reading. The '4000 holes in Blackburn, Lancashire', was picked from the Far And Near column in the *Daily Mail* dated January 17, 1967, where it was reported that a Blackburn City Council survey of road holes showed that there was one twenty-sixth of a hole in the road for each resident of the city. When John was stuck for a rhyme for 'small' to finish off the line 'Now they know how many holes it takes to fill…' his old school friend Terry Doran suggested 'the Albert Hall'.

Paul dominated *Sgt Pepper's Lonely Hearts Club Band* as John had settled into a life of casual indolence.

The band pose with the *Sgt. Pepper* cover at their manager Brian Epstein's home in west London, May 22, 1967

The film about the English army winning the war was of course *How I Won The War*, that wouldn't be premiered until October 1967 but had been talked about a lot in the press.

The man who 'blew his mind out in a car' was Tara Browne, an Irish friend of the Beatles and a well-known socialite, who died in a car accident on December 18, 1966. The coroner's report was issued in January 1967. "I didn't copy the accident," John told Hunter Davies. "Tara didn't blow his mind out. But it was in my mind when I was writing that verse." The details of the accident in the song – not noticing traffic lights and a crowd forming at the scene – were made up. Paul, who contributed lines to this part of the song, didn't know at the time that John had Tara Browne in mind. He thought he was writing about 'a stoned politician'.

Browne was driving down Redcliffe Gardens in Earls Court after midnight, when a Volkswagen emerged from a side street into his path. He swerved and his Lotus Elan ploughed into a stationary van. He was pronounced dead on arrival at a local hospital. The autopsy revealed that his death was the result of "brain lacerations due to fractures of the skull". His passenger, model Suki Potier, escaped with bruises and shock.

Tara Browne, great grandson of the brewer Edward Cecil Guinness and son of Lord Oranmore and Browne, was part of a young aristocratic elite who loved to mingle with pop stars (but he wasn't a member of the House of Lords). Although only 21 at the time of his death, he would have inherited a £1,000,000 fortune at the age of 25 and was described on his death certificate as a man "of independent means" with a London home in Eaton Row, Belgravia. After schooling at Eton, Browne married at 18 and fathered two boys before separating from his wife and taking up with Suki Potier. He frequented London nightspots such as Sibylla's and the Bag O'Nails and had become particularly friendly with Paul and Mike McCartney and Rolling Stone Brian Jones. For his 21st birthday, he had the Lovin' Spoonful flown to his ancestral home in County Wicklow, Ireland. Mick Jagger, Mike McCartney, Brian Jones and John Paul Getty were amongst the guests. Paul was with Browne when he first took LSD in 1966.

Paul's unfinished song, a bright and breezy piece about getting out of bed and setting off for school, was spliced between the second and third verses of John's song. "It was another song altogether but it happened to fit," Paul said. "It was just me remembering what it was like to run up the road to catch a bus to school, having a smoke and going into class...It was a reflection of my schooldays. I would have a Woodbine (a cheap unfiltered British cigarette) and somebody would speak and I would go into a dream."

The references to having a smoke, dreams and 'turn-ons' meant that the track was banned from the airwaves in many countries. There were even some who were convinced that the holes in Blackburn, like the holes Paul had been keen to fix, were those of a heroin user.

In 1968 Paul admitted that 'A Day In The Life' was what he called 'a turn-on song'. "This was the only one on the album written as a deliberate provocation," he said. "But what we want to do is to turn you on to the truth rather than on to pot." George Martin comments: "The 'woke up, got out of bed' bit was definitely a reference to marijuana but 'Fixing A Hole' wasn't about heroin and 'Lucy In The Sky With Diamonds' wasn't about LSD. At the time I had a strong suspicion that 'went upstairs and had a smoke' was a drug reference. They always used to disappear and have a little puff but they never did it in front of me. They always used to go down to the canteen and Mal Evans used to guard it."

A DAY IN THE LIFE
Written:
Lennon/
McCartney
Length: 5' 33"
UK release:
Sgt Pepper's Lonely Hearts Club Band album, June 1, 1967

US release:
Sgt Pepper's Lonely Hearts Club Band album, June 2, 1967

MAGICAL MYSTERY TOUR

With *Sgt Pepper* behind them, the Beatles immediately plunged into recording soundtracks for two very different films – *Yellow Submarine* and *Magical Mystery Tour*.

Yellow Submarine, a feature-length animation project, wasn't initiated by the group but they took a keen interest in its development. The Beatles were happy to see themselves turned into cartoon characters and contributed storylines as well as four original songs. The script was by a team of screenwriters, one of whom was Erich Segal, author of the best-selling novel, *Love Story*. A psychedelic fantasy, *Yellow Submarine* concerns a happy kingdom called Pepperland, which is taken over by the villainous Blue Meanies. The fab four ride to the rescue in a yellow submarine from Liverpool, eventually conquering the Meanies through the combined power of Love and Music.

Magical Mystery Tour was an experimental 50-minute colour feature for television. It started off as Paul's project but the whole group was heavily involved in all aspects of production. They financed, directed, cast and scripted the film, as well as appearing in it themselves.

Along with the single 'All You Need Is Love'/'Baby You're A Rich Man', the songs from this period are the most psychedelic of the Beatles' career. *Magical Mystery Tour* was released in America as an album in November 1967 and in Britain as a double extended-play disc in December. The *Yellow Submarine* soundtrack, which included an orchestral side from George Martin, wasn't released until January 1968, shortly after *The Beatles*.

This eclectic bunch of songs would make a fitting farewell to 1967, the year of the Summer of Love, before the more sober reflections of

The *Magical Mystery Tour* double EP was the soundtrack to an experimental TV feature that critics failed to warm to.

1968. The new year marked a fresh period in the Beatles' songwriting, when cleaning up, straightening out and getting back to basics became the order of the day.

Magical Mystery Tour, which was first seen on British television on December 26, 1967, was a critical failure, which consequently received only limited exposure in America. The music was much more successful; the British double EP reached Number 2 in the singles charts and the American album went to Number 1.

The *Yellow Submarine* film was released in July 1968 and was a commercial success in America, although it was never put on full release in Britain. The album, which featured other artists as well as the Beatles, reached the Number 3 spot in Britain and Number 2 in America.

ALL YOU NEED IS LOVE

Early in 1967, the Beatles were approached by the BBC to take part in what would be the first-ever, live global television link: a 125-minute programme broadcast to 26 countries with contributions from national broadcasting networks in Europe, Scandinavia, North America, Central America, North Africa, Japan and Australia.

To mark the occasion, the Beatles were asked to write a simple song that would be understood by viewers of all nationalities. Writing began in late May, with Paul and John working on separate compositions, until John's 'All You Need Is Love' emerged as the obvious choice. The song was not only musically and lyrically uncomplicated but also it perfectly captured the aspirations of international youth in the summer of 1967. This was the time when the war in Vietnam was at its most intense and the 'love generation' showed its opposition by staging a number of peaceful protests. "It was an inspired song and they really wanted to give the world a

---

ALL YOU NEED IS LOVE

Written:	Lennon/McCartney
Length:	3' 48"
UK single release:	July 7, 1967
UK chart position:	1
US single release:	July 17, 1967
US chart position:	1

The Beatles' plea for universal love was debuted on a 1967 TV programme that was simultaneously shown in 26 countries.

message," said Brian Epstein. "The nice thing about it is that it cannot be misinterpreted. It is a clear message saying that love is everything."

In calling for universal love, 'All You Need Is Love' extended the message that John had first tried to put across in 'The Word' in 1965. He was fascinated by the power of slogans to unite people and was determined to create something with the timelessness of 'We Shall Overcome' (a labour union song popularized in the Sixties by folk singer Pete Seeger). When asked in 1971 whether songs like 'Give Peace A Chance' and 'Power To The People' were propaganda songs, he answered, "Sure. So was 'All You Need Is Love'.. I'm a revolutionary artist. My art is dedicated to change."

The viewers of *Our World* on June 25, 1967 saw a re-creation of a Beatles recording session: rhythm tracks had been laid down on June 14 and the live input was instantaneously added and mixed for transmission. A party atmosphere was created in Abbey Road's Studio One by inviting Mick Jagger, Marianne Faithfull, Eric Clapton and Keith Moon to hold balloons, wave placards and join in on the chorus. George Martin accentuated the message of international unity by opening the song with bars from La Marseillaise (France), and closing it with snatches from 'In The Mood' (America) the Brandenburg concerto (Germany) and 'Greensleeves' (England).

The single was released on July 7, and became the anthem of the Summer of Love, a paean to peace, love and understanding. "We had been told that we'd be seen recording it by the whole world at the same time," said Paul. "So we had one message for the world – love. We need more love in the world."

BABY YOU'RE A RICH MAN

As with 'A Day In The Life', two unfinished songs were sewn together to create 'Baby You're A Rich Man', which opens with John's section, originally titled 'One Of The Beautiful People', and then moves up a gear for Paul's 'rich man' chorus.

'The beautiful people' was a term applied to the hip in-crowd who, with their long hair, free love and dope, created an alternative to 'straight' society. They used the word 'beautiful' freely in their conversations to describe anything of which they approved. "At the back of my mind somewhere...there is something which tells me that everything is beautiful," said Paul in a stoned interview with *International Times* in January 1967. "Instead of opposing things like 'Oh, I don't like that television show' or 'No, I don't like the theatre' I know really that it's all great and that everything's great and there's no bad ever if I can think of it all as great."

In 1967, San Francisco was regarded as the city of the beautiful people because it was here that the hippy movement was first spotted by the media and where the first psychedelic 'happenings' and open-air 'tribal gatherings' had taken place. Although the Beatles played San Francisco in 1964, 1965 and 1966, they didn't really get to explore the city until 1967. Paul was the first to visit, on April 4, when he dropped in on a Jefferson Airplane rehearsal and jammed on guitar. George was next, on August 7, when he came to Haight Ashbury, the San Francisco district that had given birth to underground newspapers, psychedelic poster art, communes, crash pads, head shops, free clinics and legions of exotic street people. Pattie's sister Jenny was living in the area. "You are our leader, George," one hippy shouted as he set off walking from the corner

**BABY, YOU'RE
A RICH MAN
Written:**
Lennon/
McCartney
Length: 3' 03"
UK single release:
July 7, 1967 as
B-side of 'All You
Need Is Love'
US single release:
July 17, 1967 as
B-side of 'All You
Need Is Love'

of Haight and Masonic with Pattie, Neil Aspinall and Derek Taylor beside him. "You know where it's at."

George was taken aback at the drug-glazed adoration of those who pushed flowers, poems, posters and drugs at him. "It's you who should be leading yourself," he told his would-be followers. "You don't want to be following leaders – me or anyone else." When he arrived at a park, George sat on the grass, listened to other people's songs and then started to sing 'Baby You're A Rich Man'.

The rich man in Paul's section is reputed to be manager Brian Epstein and in a demo version of the song, John maligns him by singing 'Baby, you're a rich fag Jew'. "The point was," said John, "stop moaning. You're a rich man and we're all rich men."

Paul may have used the Beatles' manager, Brian Epstein, as the 'rich man' of 'Baby You're A Rich Man'.

HELLO GOODBYE

Alistair Taylor, Brian Epstein's assistant, remembered once asking Paul how he wrote his songs, and Paul took him into his dining room to give a demonstration on a hand-carved harmonium. He told Taylor to shout out the opposite of whatever he sang as he struck the keys. And so it went – black and white, yes and no, stop and go, hello and goodbye. "I've no memory at all of the tune," Taylor later recounted. "You have to remember that melodies are as common around the Beatles as bugs in May. Some grow into bright butterflies and others shrivel and die. I wonder whether Paul really made up that song as he went along or whether it was running through his head already. Anyway, shortly afterwards, he arrived at the office with a demo tape of the latest single – 'Hello Goodbye.'"

The last part of the record, where the Beatles repeat the line 'Hela, hey, aloha' came about spontaneously in the studio. ('Aloha' is an affectionate form of Hawaiian greeting.)

If 'Hello Goodbye' was nothing more than a word game set to music, in the mystical climate of 1967, Paul was expected to offer a deeper interpretation. In an interview with *Disc*, he gallantly tried to produce an explanation: "the answer to everything is simple. It's a song about everything and nothing…to have white. That's the amazing thing about life."

'Hello Goodbye' was released as a single in November 1967 and topped the charts in both Britain and America. The final 'aloha' chorus was used in the *Magical Mystery Tour* film.

George expressed his resentment at the financial set-up of publishing company Northern Songs in 'Only A Northern Song' (right).

HELLO GOODBYE
Written: Lennon/ McCartney
Length: 3' 31"
UK single release: November 24, 1967
UK chart position: 1
US single release: November 27, 1967
US chart position: 1

ONLY A NORTHERN SONG

Originally recorded in February 1967 as George's contribution to *Sgt Pepper's Lonely Hearts Club Band*, 'Only A Northern Song' first saw the light of day in *Yellow Submarine*. The song was a sly dig at the business arrangements of the Beatles. Their songs had always been published by Northern Songs Ltd, 30 per cent of whose shares belonged to John and Paul, with Ringo and George owning only 1.6 per cent each. This meant that John and Paul, in addition to being the group's main songwriters, were benefiting again as prime shareholders in the publishing company. As far as Northern Songs was concerned, George was a merely a contracted writer.

In 'Only A Northern Song', George complained that it didn't really matter what he wrote because the bulk of the money was going into other people's pockets. Underlying this was his feeling, only expressed publicly after the group had broken up, that his songs were being ignored and that he his contributions were used as mere tokens.

"At first it was just great (to get one song on each album), it was like, hey, I'm getting in on the act too!" George commented. "After a while I did (come to resent this), especially when I had good songs. Sometimes I had songs that were better than some of their songs and we'd have to record maybe eight of theirs before they'd *listen* to one of mine."

It's not surprising that George, who in 1964 claimed "security is the only thing I want. Money to do nothing with, money to have in case you want to do something", ultimately became the Beatle least keen to resurrect the Beatles.

45

ONLY A NORTHERN SONG
Written:
Harrison
Length: 3' 27"
UK release:
Yellow Submarine album, January 17, 1969
US release:
Yellow Submarine album, January 13, 1969

ALL TOGETHER NOW

Paul, Ringo and George pose with a cardboard cut-out of John at the July 1968 press launch of their *Yellow Submarine* animated movie.

'All Together Now' was written in the studio in May 1967 with Paul as main contributor. It was intended as another 'Yellow Submarine' and John was delighted later when he heard that British soccer crowds were singing it.

One of the effects of psychedelia was a renewed interest in the innocence of childhood and nursery rhymes would begin to affect their post-Pepper work. Folklorist Iona Opie, editor of *The Oxford Dictionary of Nursery Rhymes*, believes that as the lines sound so familiar, it draws more on a shared memory: "I can't distinguish any particular influence on 'All Together Now'," she says. "So many ABC rhymes exist and there are counting rhymes like 'One, two, three, four, Mary at the cottage door...' which come pretty close. The song seems to come out of a universal subconscious."

Paul has confirmed that he saw it in the tradition of children's songs ("It's a *Play Away* command song") but that he was also playing with the dual meaning of 'all together now' which could be either a music-hall-style invitation to participate or a slogan for world unity. Paul Horn remembers the song being sung while they were in India but instead of singing 'H, I, J, I love you' they would sing 'H, I, Jai Guru Dev' in honour of Maharishi's spiritual master.

ALL TOGETHER NOW
Written:
Lennon/
McCartney
Length: 2' 13"
UK release:
Yellow Submarine
album, January 17,
1969
US release:
Yellow Submarine
album, January 13,
1969

HEY BULLDOG

'Hey Bulldog' was recorded on February 11, 1968, when the Beatles were at Abbey Road to make a promotional film for 'Lady Madonna'. Paul suggested that instead of wasting time pretending to record 'Lady Madonna', they should tape something new and so John produced some unfinished lyrics he'd written for *Yellow Submarine*. John explained to the others how he heard the song and they all threw in suggestions for the words. One line John had written – 'Some kind of solitude is measured out in news' – was misread and came out as 'Some kind of solitude is measured out in you'. They decided to keep it.

The bulldog of the title never existed before the recording. The original lyric mentioned a bullfrog but, to everyone's amusement, Paul started to bark at the end of the song. Because of this, they retitled it.

Erich Segal, the author of *Love Story*, was one of the screenwriters on *Yellow Submarine*. Years later, he claimed that 'Hey Bulldog' had been written for him because the bulldog was the mascot of Yale University where he was a lecturer in classics!

HEY BULLDOG	
Written:	Lennon/McCartney
Length:	3' 14"
UK release:	*Yellow Submarine* album, January 17, 1969
US release:	*Yellow Submarine* album, January 13, 1969

IT'S ALL TOO MUCH

George was the Beatle who most often spoke in spiritual terms about his experience of LSD. 'It's All Too Much', recorded in May 1967, was written, George said, "in a childlike manner from realizations that appeared during and after some LSD experiences and which were later confirmed in meditation".

Through images of silver suns and streaming time, the song attempted to articulate the feeling of personal identity being swallowed up by a benign force. Three months after this recording, George met the Maharishi Mahesh Yogi and began to view his LSD experience as a signpost rather than a destination. "LSD isn't a real answer," he said in September 1967. "It doesn't give you anything. It enables you to see a lot of possibilities that you may never have noticed before but it isn't the answer. It can help you go from A to B, but when you get to B you see C, and you see that to get really high, you have to do it straight. There are special ways of getting high without drugs – with yoga, meditation and all those things."

Paul stands by the bus that loomed large in the *Magical Mystery Tour* TV special.

IT'S ALL TOO MUCH

Written:	Harrison
Length:	6' 28"
UK release:	*Yellow Submarine* album, January 17, 1969
US release:	*Yellow Submarine* album, January 13, 1969

MAGICAL MYSTERY TOUR

Flying home to London on April 11, 1967, after visiting Jane Asher in Denver for her 21st birthday party, Paul began to work on an idea for a Beatles television special. The group felt that they had outgrown the 'caper' format which had made them such a big hit in the cinema and now Paul was keen to make films himself, working with an 8mm camera and composing electronic soundtracks.

Encouraged by the experimental mood of the times, Paul envisaged making an unscripted film where characters and locations were chosen in advance , but the story was improvised on camera. His plan was to put the Beatles alongside an assorted collection of actors and colourful characters on a strange coach journey through the English countryside.

As Hunter Davies reported in the *Sunday Times* the day before *Magical Mystery Tour* was shown on British television: "(They had decided that the film) would be Magical, so that they could do any ideas which came to them, and Mysterious in that neither they nor the rest of the passengers would know what they were going to do

---

MAGICAL MYSTERY TOUR

Written:	Lennon/McCartney
Length:	2' 51"
UK release:	'Magical Mystery Tour' EP, December 8, 1967
US release:	*Magical Mystery Tour* album, November 27, 1967

next…'The whole thing will be a mystery to everyone,' Paul told the rest of the Beatles, 'including us.'"

There were two main inspirations behind *Magical Mystery Tour*. The first was the British working-class custom of the 'mystery tour', an organized day trip by coach, where only the driver knows the destination. The second was American novelist Ken Kesey's idea of driving through America on a psychedelically painted bus. The sign on the front of Kesey's bus read 'Furthur' (sic) and the one on the back – 'Caution. Weird load'. The bus was full of counter-culture 'freaks' who Kesey fed loud music and copious amounts of drugs just to see what would happen. His driver was Neal Cassady, the model for Dean Moriarty in Jack Kerouac's *On The Road*. The story of their adventures was eventually told in Tom Wolfe's book *The Electric Kool-Aid Acid Test*.

The Beatles were aware of Kesey's activities and later, when the Apple record label was founded, Kesey visited the office in Savile Row to record a spoken-word album.

On April 25, Paul arrived at Abbey Road studios with nothing more than the song title, the first line and a general idea for the tune. He said he wanted his new song to be like a commercial for the television programme, letting viewers know what was in store. Mal Evans was dispatched to find some real mystery tour posters from which they could lift phrases but, after visiting coach stations, returned empty-handed. When the backing track had been recorded, Paul asked everyone to shout out words connected with mystery tours which Mal wrote down. They came up with 'invitation', 'reservation', 'trip of a lifetime' and 'satisfaction guaranteed', but it wasn't enough and so the vocal track was filled with gobbledy-gook until Paul returned two days later with a completed lyric.

Paul's words were a mixture of traditional fairground barking and contemporary drug references. To the majority of the audience 'roll up, roll up' was the ringmasters invitation to the circus. To Paul it was also an invitation to roll up a joint. The Magical Mystery Tour was going to 'take you away', on a trip. Even the phrase 'dying to take you away' was a conscious reference to the *Tibetan Book Of The Dead*.

The track was used over an opening sequence made up of scenes from the film with an additional spoken section which declared: "When a man buys a ticket for a magical mystery tour, he knows what to expect. We guarantee him the trip of a lifetime, and that's just what he gets – the incredible Magical Mystery Tour."

"On yer 'ed!" George and Paul and take a break from filming on the set of *Magical Mystery Tour*.

FOOL ON THE HILL

Paul started work on 'Fool On The Hill' in March 1967 while he was writing 'With A Little Help From My Friends', although it wasn't recorded until September.

Paul's encounter with a mysterious stranger on London's Primrose Hill was indirectly to lead to 'Fool On The Hill'.

Hunter Davies observed Paul singing and playing "a very slow, beautiful song about a foolish man sitting on the hill", while John listened staring blankly out of the window at Cavendish Avenue. "Paul sang it many times, la la-ing words he hadn't thought of yet. When at last he finished, John said he'd better write the words down or he'd forget them. Paul said it was OK. He wouldn't forget them," comments Davies.

The song was about an idiot savant, a person everyone considers to be a fool but who is actually a misunderstood visionary. Paul was thinking of gurus like Maharishi Mahesh Yogi who were often derided and an Italian hermit he once read about who emerged from a cave in the late 1940s to discover that he'd missed the entire Second World War. An experience which is said to have contributed to Paul's image of the fool standing on the hill is recounted by Alistair Taylor in his book *Yesterday*.

Taylor recalls an early morning walk on Primrose Hill with Paul and his dog Martha, where they watched the sun rise before realizing that Martha had gone missing. "We turned round to go and suddenly there he was standing behind us," wrote Taylor. "He was a middle-aged man, very respectably dressed in a belted raincoat. Nothing in that, you may think, but he'd come up behind us over the bare top of the hill in total silence."

Both Paul and Taylor were sure that the man hadn't been there seconds earlier because they'd been searching the area for the dog.

FOOL ON THE HILL

Written:	Lennon/McCartney
Length:	3' 00"
UK release:	'Magical Mystery Tour' EP, December 8, 1967
US release:	*Magical Mystery Tour* album, November 27, 1967

He seemed to have appeared miraculously. The three men exchanged greetings, the man commented on the beautiful view and then walked way. When they looked around, he'd vanished. "There was no sign of the man," said Taylor. " He'd just disappeared from the top of the hill as if he'd been carried off into the air! No one could have run to the thin cover of the nearest trees in the time we had turned away from him, and no one could have run over the crest of the hill."

What added to the mystery was that immediately before the man's appearance Paul and Taylor had, provoked by the beautiful view over London and the rising of the sun, been mulling over the existence of God. "Paul and I both felt the same weird sensation that something special had happened. We sat down rather shakily on the seat and Paul said, 'What the hell do you make of that? That's weird. He was here, wasn't he? We did speak to him?'

"Back at Cavendish, we spent the rest of the morning talking about what we had seen and heard and felt," continues Taylor. "It sounds just like any acid tripper's fantasy to say they had a religious experience on Primrose Hill just before the morning rush hour, but neither of us had taken anything like that. Scotch and Coke was the only thing we'd touched all night. We both felt we'd been through some mystical religious experience, yet we didn't care to name even to each other what or who we'd seen on that hilltop for those few brief seconds."

In *Magical Mystery Tour*, the song was used over a sequence with Paul on a hilltop overlooking Nice.

FLYING

The Beatles had recorded two previous instrumentals – 'Cry For A Shadow' in Germany in 1961 (when backing Tony Sheridan as the Beat Brothers) and the unreleased '12-Bar Original' in 1965. 'Flying' was the only instrumental to be released on a Beatles' record.

Used as incidental music for *Magical Mystery Tour*, 'Flying' emerged out of a studio jam. Originally titled 'Aerial Tour Instrumental', it was registered as a group composition and featured a basic rhythm track with additional mellotron, backwards organ and vocal chanting. The cloud scenes over which 'Flying' was heard in the film, were originally shot by Stanley Kubrick for *2001 Space Odyssey* but never used.

FLYING
Written:
Harrison/Lennon/
McCartney
Length: 2' 16"
UK release:
'Magical Mystery
Tour' EP,
December 8, 1967
US release:
*Magical Mystery
Tour* album,
November 27,
1967

George waiting to film the 'Blue Jay Way' sequence of *Magical Mystery Tour*.

BLUE JAY WAY

BLUE JAY WAY
Written:
Harrison
Length: 3' 56"
UK release:
'Magical Mystery
Tour' EP,
December 8,
1967
US release:
*Magical Mystery
Tour* album,
November 27,
1967

'Blue Jay Way' was written by George in August 1967 during his visit to California with Pattie, Neil Aspinall and Alex Mardas. On arrival in Los Angeles on August 1, they were driven to a small rented cottage with a pool on Blue Jay Way, a street high in the Hollywood Hills above Sunset Boulevard. It belonged to Robert Fitzpatrick, a music business lawyer who was on vacation in Hawaii.

Derek Taylor, formerly the Beatles' press officer and now a publicist working in Los Angeles, was due to visit them on their first night in town, but got lost in the narrow canyons on his way to the cottage, and was delayed. There was a small Hammond organ in the corner of the room and George whiled away the time by composing a song about being stuck in a house on Blue Jay Way while his friends were lost in the fog.

Blue Jay Way is a notoriously hard street to find – you can be geographically close and yet separated by a ravine. "By the time we got there the song was virtually intact," says Derek Taylor. "Of course, at the time I felt very bad. Here were these two wretchedly jet-lagged people and we were about two hours late. But here, indeed, was a song which turned up in *Magical Mystery Tour* (the film) through a prism with about eight images, with George in a red jacket sitting and playing piano on the floor."

Taylor was amused by what people made of the song. One critic thought the line in which George urged his guest not to 'be long' was advice to young people telling them not to 'belong' (to society, that is). Another acclaimed musicologist believed that, when George said that his friends had 'lost their way', he meant that a whole generation had lost direction. "It's just a simple little song," says Taylor.

YOUR MOTHER SHOULD KNOW

'Your Mother Should Know' by Paul could have been written as early as May 1967, when both John and Paul were working on songs for the *Our World* television special. Like 'When I'm 64', the song was a tribute to the music his father enjoyed singing when he was a young man in Jim Mac's Jazz Band. Jim McCartney formed his own ragtime band in 1919 and played dates around Liverpool, performing numbers like 'Birth Of The Blues' and 'Stairway To Paradise'. One day, Paul surprised his dad by recording one of his compositions under the title 'Walking In The Park With Eloise', under the alias of the Country Hams.

Paul wrote it at Cavendish Avenue and thinks it was affected by the fact that his Auntie Gin and Uncle Harry were staying with him at the time. It was the sort of song that they would have liked. Paul also had in mind the idea of 'mother knows best', a lament for those who were no longer close to their parents.

'Your Mother Should Know', however, found its way into the *Magical Mystery Tour* in a scene where the four Beatles, in white tail suits, descend a staircase and are joined by teams of formation dancers. Strictly speaking, any hit that Paul's mother would have known would have been a hit before she was born in 1909, in the days when hits were not determined by record sales but by sales of sheet music.

Paul and John may have written 'Your Mother Should Know' as early as May 1967.

> **YOUR MOTHER SHOULD KNOW**
> **Written:** Lennon/ McCartney
> **Length:** 2' 29"
> **UK release:** 'Magical Mystery Tour' EP, December 8, 1967
> **US release:** *Magical Mystery Tour* album, November 27, 1967

I AM THE WALRUS

The sprawling, disjointed nature of 'I Am The Walrus' owes much to the fact that it is an amalgamation of at least three song ideas that John was working on, none of which seemed quite enough in its own right. The first, inspired by hearing a distant police siren while at home in Weybridge, started with the words 'Mis-ter c-ity police-man' and fitted the rhythm of the siren. The second was a pastoral melody about his Weybridge garden. The third was a nonsense song about sitting on a corn flake.

John told Hunter Davies, who was still researching the Beatles' official biography at the time: "I don't know how it will all end up. Perhaps they'll turn out to be different parts of the same song." According to Pete Shotton, the final catalyst was a letter received from a pupil of Quarry Bank School, which mentioned that an English master was getting his class to analyze Beatles' songs. The letter from the Quarry Bank pupil was sent to John by Stephen Bayley who received an answer dated September 1, 1967 (which was sold at auction by Christie's of London in 1992). This amused John, who decided to confuse such people with a song full of the most perplexing and incoherent clues. He asked Shotton to remind him of a silly playground rhyme which English schoolchildren at the time delighted in. John wrote it down: 'Yellow matter custard, green slop pie, All mixed together with a dead dog's eye, Slap it on a butty, ten foot thick, Then wash it all down with a cup of cold sick'.

John proceeded to invent some ludicrous images ('semolina pilchards, elementary penguins') and nonsense words ('texpert, crabalocker'), before adding some opening lines he'd written down during an acid trip. He then strung these together with the three

Allen Ginsberg was mocked by John as an 'elementary penguin' in the typically acerbic 'I Am The Walrus'.

unfinished songs he'd already shown Hunter Davies. "Let the fuckers work that one out", he apparently said to Shotton when he'd finished. Asked by *Playboy* to explain 'Walrus' some 13 years later, he remarked that he thought Dylan got away with murder at times and that he'd decided "I can write this crap too."

The only serious part of the lyric, apparently, was the opening line with its vision of the unity behind all things.

The 'elementary penguin' which chanted 'Hare Krishna' was John having a dig at Allen Ginsberg who, at the time, was chanting the Hare Krishna mantra at public events. The walrus itself came from Lewis Carroll's poem 'The Walrus and the Carpenter'.

The 'eggman' was supposedly a reference to Animals' vocalist Eric Burdon who had an unusual practice of breaking eggs over his female conquests while making love and became known among his musical colleagues as the 'egg man'. Marianne Faithfull believes that 'semolina pilchard' was a reference to Det. Sgt. Norman Pilcher, the Metropolitan police officer who made a name for himself by targeting pop stars for drug possession.

The recording of 'I Am The Walrus' began on September 5. It lasted on and off throughout the month because George Martin was trying to find an equivalent to the flow of images and word play in the lyrics by using violins, cellos, horns, clarinet and a 16-voice choir, in addition to the Beatles themselves. On September 29, some lines from Shakespeare (*King Lear* Act IV Scene VI) were fed into the song from a BBC broadcast.

I AM THE WALRUS
Written: Lennon/ McCartney
Length: 4' 37"
UK single release: November 24, 1967 as B-side to 'Hello Goodbye'
US single release: November 27, 1967 as B-side to 'Hello Goodbye'

LADY MADONNA

'Lady Madonna' was the first single to show that the way forward for the Beatles now lay in returning to the basic rock'n'roll of their early days. After *Sgt Pepper's Lonely Hearts Club Band* and *Magical Mystery Tour*, it was assumed that musical progression would mean more complexity, but the Beatles again defied expectations.

The main riff was taken from Johnny Parker's piano playing on the instrumental 'Bad Penny Blues', a 1956 hit in Britain for jazz trumpeter Humphrey Lyttelton and his band, that had been produced by George Martin. "We asked George how they got the sound on 'Bad Penny Blues'," said Ringo. "George told us that they used brushes. So I used brushes and we did a track with just brushes and piano and then we decided we needed an off-beat, so we put an off-beat in." Lyttelton didn't mind at all, as Parker had taken the riff from Dan Burley anyway. "You can't copyright a rhythm and rhythm was all that they had borrowed," he said. "I was very complimented. Although none of the

---

LADY MADONNA

Written:	Lennon/McCartney
Length:	2' 18"
UK single release:	March 15, 1968
UK chart position:	1
US single release:	March 18, 1968
US chart position:	4

Beatles cared for traditional jazz, they all knew and liked 'Bad Penny Blues' because it was a bluesy, skiffley thing rather than a trad exercise." (Dan Burley and His Skiffle Boys, formed in 1946, was the source of the description 'skiffle music' first applied to the folk-blues-country style of Lonnie Donegan in Britain during the early 1950s.)

The song was intended by Paul to be a celebration of motherhood which started with an image of the Virgin Mary but then moved on to consider all mothers. "How do they do it?", he asked when interviewed by *Musician* in 1986. "Baby at your breast – how do they get the time to feed them? Where do they get the money? How do you do this thing that women do?"

The singer Richie Havens remembered being with Paul in a Greenwich Village club when a girl came up to him and asked whether 'Lady Madonna' had been written about America. "No," said Paul. "I was looking through this African magazine and I saw this African lady with a baby. And underneath the picture it said 'Mountain Madonna'. But I said, oh no – Lady Madonna – and I wrote the song."

Released as a single in March 1968, 'Lady Madonna' went to Number 1 in Britain but stalled at Number 4 in America.

After the psychedelic stylings of *Magical Mystery Tour*, the Beatles returned to the basic rock 'n' roll of their early tours with 'Lady Madonna'.

THE INNER LIGHT

On September 29, 1967, John and George were guests of David Frost on the live late-night television show *The Frost Report*. The subject of this edition was Transcendental Meditation and it included an interview with the Maharishi Mahesh Yogi, filmed earlier the same day at London Airport.

In the invited audience at the studio in Wembley, north London was Sanskrit scholar Juan Mascaró, a Cambridge professor. The following month, Mascaró wrote to George enclosing a copy of *Lamps Of Fire*, a collection of spiritual wisdom from various traditions that he had edited. He suggested that George might consider putting verses from the Tao Te Ching to music, in particular a poem titled 'The Inner Light'.

In his preface to *Lamps Of Fire*, first published in 1958, Mascaró wrote: "The passages of this book are lamps of fire. Some shine more and some shine less, but they all merge into that vast lamp called by St John of the Cross 'the lamp of the being of God'."

'The Inner Light' was the first song of George's to appear on a single when it became the B side of 'Lady Madonna'.

THE INNER LIGHT
Written:
Harrison
Length: 2' 36"
UK single release:
March 15, 1968 as
B-side to 'Lady
Madonna'
US single release:
March 18, 1968 as
B-side to 'Lady
Madonna'

HEY JUDE

As John and Yoko started living together, not surprisingly, divorce proceedings began between John and Cynthia. An interim agreement was reached whereby Cynthia and Julian were allowed to stay at Kenwood while the two respondents took up residence in a Montagu Square flat in central London.

Paul had always enjoyed a close relationship with John's son Julian, then five years old and, to show support for mother and child during the break-up, he drove down to Weybridge from his home in St John's Wood bearing a single red rose. Paul often used driving time to work out new songs and, on this day, with Julian's uncertain future on his mind, he started singing 'Hey Julian' and improvising lyrics on the theme of comfort and reassurance. At some point during the hour-long journey, 'Hey Julian' became 'Hey Jules' and Paul developed the lines 'Hey Jules, don't make it bad, Take a sad song and make it better'. It was only later, when he came to flesh out the lyric, that he changed Jules to Jude, feeling that Jude was a name that sounded stronger. He had liked the name Jud when he'd seen the musical *Oklahoma*.

The song then became less specific. John believed it was addressed to him, encouraging him to make the break from the Beatles and build a new future with Yoko ('You were made to go out and get her…'). Paul felt that, if it was addressed to anyone, it was to himself, dealing with the adjustments he knew that he was going to have to make as old bonds were broken within the Beatles.

The music drove the lyric, with sound taking precedence over sense. One line in particular – 'the movement you need is on your shoulder' – was intended as a temporary filler. When Paul played the song to John, he pointed out that this line needed replacing, saying it sounded as if he was singing about his parrot. "It's probably the best line in the song," said John. "Leave it in. I know what it means."

Julian Lennon grew up knowing the story behind 'Hey Jude' but it wasn't until 1987 that he heard the facts first-hand from Paul, whom he bumped into in New York. "It was the first time in years that we'd sat down and talked to each other," says Julian. "He told me that he'd been thinking about my circumstances all those years ago, about what I was going through and what I would have to go through in the future. Paul and I used to hang out quite a bit – more than dad and I did. Maybe Paul was into kids a bit more at the time. We had a great friendship going and there seem to be far more pictures of me and Paul playing together at that age than pictures of me and dad."

"I've never really wanted to know the truth about how dad was and how he was with me," Julian admits. "I kept my mouth shut. There was some very negative stuff talked about me – like when he said that I'd come out of a whisky bottle on a Saturday night. Stuff like that. That's tough to deal with. You think, where's the love in that? It was very psychologically damaging and for years that affected me. I used to think, how could he say that about his own bloody son!"

Julian hasn't studied the words of 'Hey Jude' for some time but finds it hard to get away from the song. He'll be in a restaurant when he'll hear it played, or it'll come on the car radio when he's driving. "It surprises me whenever I hear it," he says. "It's very strange to think that someone has written a song about you. It still touches me."

'Hey Jude' was the most successful Beatles' single ever. It topped the charts around the world and, before the end of 1967, over five million copies had been sold.

HEY JUDE

Written:	Lennon/McCartney
Length:	7' 08"
UK single release:	August 30, 1968
UK chart position:	1
US single release:	August 26, 1968
US chart position:	1

THE BEATLES

The Beatles, or *The White Album* as it is commonly referred to,, confounded expectations because of its simplicity. It was as if the group had decided to produce the exact opposite of *Sgt Pepper.* Long album title? Let's just call it *The Beatles.* Multi-coloured cover? Let's go white. Clever overdubs and mixes? Let's use acoustic guitars on a lot of the tracks. Other-worldly subject matter? Let's sing about cowboys, pigs, chocolates and doing it in the road.

The change was in part due to the Beatles' interest in the teachings of Indian guru, Maharishi Mahesh Yogi. Pattie Harrison had attended a lecture given by him in February 1967 and six months later she encouraged George and the rest of the Beatles to hear him speak at the Hilton Hotel in Park Lane, London. As a result of this meeting, they all embarked on a ten-day course on Transcendental Meditation, at University College, Bangor, in North Wales.

While in Bangor, on Sunday, August 27, 1967, they learned that Brian Epstein had been found dead at his Belgravia flat. The loss of Epstein, who had managed their career since early 1962 and had become something of a father figure, may well have made the Beatles even more open to the guidance of the Maharishi, whom they visited in India in February 1968.

The trip to India not only brought calm and self-reflection to their fraught lives but also rekindled their musical friendships. Paul Horn, an American flautist who was there at the same time, believes that meditation was a great stimulus for them. "You find out more about yourself on deeper levels when you're meditating," he said. "Look how prolific they were in such a relatively short time. They were in the Himalayas away from the pressures and away from the

The time spent in India under the guidance of Maharishi Mahesh Yogi gave the Beatles the breathing space to write the follow-up to *Sgt Pepper*.

telephone. When you get too involved with life, it suppresses your creativity. When you're able to be quiet, it starts coming up."

On their return from India, the Beatles claimed that they had brought back 30 songs which they would be using on their next album. There were indeed 30 new songs on *The Beatles* but not all of them were written in India, and some of the Indian songs (like George's 'Sour Milk Sea' and 'Circles') were never recorded by the Beatles. It's probably fairer to say that about half of the album was written or at least started while they were away. Because they had no access to electric guitars or keyboards, many of these songs were acoustic.

John would later refer to *The Beatles* as being the first unself-conscious album after the Beatles' great period of self-consciousness beginning with *Rubber Soul* and ending with *Magical Mystery Tour* and *Yellow Submarine*. *The Beatles* was released as a double album in November 1968 and rose to the Number 1 spot on both sides of the Atlantic.

BACK IN THE USSR

Friendly rivalry existed between the Beatles and the Beach Boys, and between 1965 and 1968 each new effort by either band spurred the other on to greater heights. When Brian Wilson heard *Rubber Soul*, he reported that it blew his mind to hear an album of such variety and consistency. "It flipped me out so much," he said, "that I determined to try the same thing – to make an entire album that was a gas." His reply was *Pet Sounds*, the Beach Boys' crowning achievement, which contained 'Sloop John B', 'Caroline No', 'Wouldn't It Be Nice' and 'God Only Knows'. When Paul heard *Pet Sounds*, he was equally impressed and the influence could be heard on *Revolver* and *Sgt Pepper*.

Although they admired each other, the two groups had little social contact. Carl Wilson and Mike Love had seen the Beatles play in Portland, Oregon, on August 22, 1965, and called by the dressing room after the show. Brian Johnson had been present at the Waldorf Hotel in London when John and Paul were played a pressing of *Pet Sounds* in April 1966 and in April 1967, Paul dropped by the studios in LA where Brian Wilson was working on the Beach Boys track 'Vegetables'.

The most prolonged contact came in February 1968, when all four Beatles and their partners travelled to Rishikesh, India, to study Transcendental Meditation under the Maharishi Mahesh Yogi. On the course were three other professional musicians – Scottish singer Donovan, American flautist Paul Horn and Beach Boy Mike Love. The musicians spent a great deal of time together talking, jamming and songwriting.

One of the songs that came out of this encounter was 'Back In The USSR', written by Paul as a pastiche of the Beach Boys and

The Beach Boys and the Beatles constantly strove to outperform each other.

Chuck Berry. The genesis of the song was a comment made by Love to Paul one morning over breakfast. "Wouldn't it be fun to do a Soviet version of 'Back In The USA'," Love suggested, referring to Berry's jingoistic 1959 single in which the singer expressed how mighty glad he was to be back home in civilized America with its cafes, drive-ins, skyscrapers, hamburgers and juke boxes. The Beach Boys had earlier drawn on this song and Berry's 'Sweet Sixteen' for their tracks 'California Girls' and 'Surfin' USA', in which they extolled the virtues of local ladies and surf beaches.

Paul acted on Love's suggestion and came up with a parody that did for the USSR what Berry had done for the USA and for Soviet women what the Beach Boys had done for the girls of California. After a decade of songs which had made poetry out of the names of places such as Memphis, Chicago and New Orleans, it was striking to hear Moscow mentioned in rock'n'roll. "I just liked the idea of Georgia girls and talking about places like the Ukraine as if it was California," said Paul. As a tribute to Love, the Beatles' eventual recording imitated the vocal harmonies of the Beach Boys.

In a radio interview given in November 1968 Paul said, "In my mind it's just about a (Russian) spy who's been in America for a long time and he's become very American but when he gets back to the USSR he's saying 'Leave it 'til tomorrow to unpack my case, Honey, disconnect the phone.' and all that, but to Russian women."

'Back In The USSR' disturbed conservative Americans, because at a time of Cold War and conflict in Vietnam it appeared to be

'Back In The USSR' led some right-wing US commentators to condemn the band as communist subversives

celebrating the enemy. Having admitted to drug-taking, were these long-haired boys now embracing communism? American anti-rock campaigner David A Noebel, author of *Communism, Hypnotism and the Beatles*, while unable to produce their party membership cards, was sure that they were furthering the cause of revolutionary socialism. "John Lennon and the Beatles were an integral part of the revolutionary milieu and received high marks from the Communist press," he wrote, "especially for the *White Album* which contained 'Back In The USSR' and 'Piggies'. One line from 'Back In The USSR' left the anti-Communists speechless: 'You don't know how lucky you are boy/Back in the USSR.'"

Through more diligent research, Noebel would have discovered that the official Soviet line was that the Beatles were evidence of capitalism's decadence. Just as the Nazis declared jazz music and abstract painting 'degenerate' so the Communists railed against the evil of rock'n'roll and promoted folk music that extolled the virtues of the State. Young people in the Soviet Union were just as excited by the Beatles' music as their Western counterparts but had to rely on bootleg recordings, smuggled imports and radio broadcasts from America and Britain. In 1988, with the Cold War about to be consigned to history, Paul paid tribute to his Soviet fans by recording an album of rock'n'roll standards on the official government recording label, Melodia. In May 2003 he played a concert in Red Square and had a private meeting at the Kremlin with Vladimir Putin who told him that he had listened to Beatles music as a teenager. "It was very popular," he told Paul. "More than popular. It was a breath of fresh air, a window onto the outside world."

"'Back In The USSR' is a hands-across-the-water song," said Paul in 1968. "They like us out there. Even though the bosses in the Kremlin may not, the kids do."

BACK IN THE USSR
Written: Lennon/ McCartney
Length: 2' 43"
UK release: *The Beatles* album, November 22, 1968
US release: *The Beatles* album, November 25, 1968

DEAR PRUDENCE

Prudence was Prudence Farrow (younger sister of the American actress Mia Farrow) who attended the same course with the Beatles in India. The song was a plea to her to come out from her excessively long periods of meditation and relax with the rest of the group.

At the end of the demo version of 'Dear Prudence', John continues playing guitar and says: "No one was to know that sooner or later she was to go completely berserk, under the care of Maharishi Mahesh Yogi. All the people around were very worried about the girl because she was going insane. So, we sang to her." Later, John was to explain that Prudence had gone slightly 'barmy', locked in her room meditating for three weeks, "trying to reach God quicker than anyone else".

Paul Horn, the American flautist, says that Prudence was a highly sensitive person and that, by jumping straight into deep meditation, against the Maharishi's advice, she had allowed herself to fall into a catatonic state. "She was ashen-white and didn't recognize anybody," he says. "She didn't even recognize her own brother, who was on the course with her. The only person she showed any slight recognition towards was Maharishi. We were all very concerned about her and Maharishi assigned her a full-time nurse."

Prudence, whose living quarters were in the same building as the four Beatles and their partners, denies that she went mad but agrees that she was more fanatical about meditating than the Beatles were. "I'd been meditating since 1966 and had tried to get on the course in 1967, so it was like a dream come true for me," she explains. "Being on that course was more important to me than anything in the world. I was very focused on getting in as much meditation as possible, so that I could gain enough experience to teach it myself. I knew that I must have stuck out because I would always rush straight back to my room

DEAR PRUDENCE
Written:
Lennon/
McCartney
Length: 3' 56"
UK release:
The Beatles album,
November 22,
1968
US release:
The Beatles album,
November 25,
1968

after lectures and meals so that I could meditate. It was all so fascinating to me. John, George and Paul would all want to sit around jamming and having a good time and I'd be flying into my room. They were all serious about what they were doing but they just weren't as fanatical as me. The song that John wrote was just saying, 'Come out and play with us. Come out and have fun.'"

Maharishi Mahesh Yogi was concerned about over-sensitive student Prudence Farrow.

This she eventually did and got to know the Beatles well. The Maharishi put her in an after-lecture discussion group with John and George – who he thought would be good for her. "We talked about the things we were all going through," she says. "We were questioning reality, asking questions about who we were and what was going on. I liked them and I think they liked me."

Although the song was written in India and Prudence overheard various jam sessions between the Beatles, Mike Love and Donovan, John never played the song to her. "George was the one who told me about it," she recalls. "At the end of the course, just as they were leaving, he mentioned that they had written a song about me but I didn't hear it until it came out on the album. I was flattered. It was a beautiful thing to have done."

Prudence is now married and lives in Florida where she teaches meditation. In October 1983, Siouxie and the Banshees had a British Top 10 hit with their version of 'Dear Prudence'.

GLASS ONION

In an age of rapid social change, the Beatles were often regarded as prophets and every song was scrutinized for symbols and allusions. Who was the egg man in 'I Am The Walrus'? Was the tea that was mentioned in 'Lovely Rita' really marijuana? Was 'Henry The Horse' street slang for heroin?

The Beatles had perhaps laid themselves open to this by mixing poetry with nonsense. John, in particular, had enjoyed obfuscating his point of view, perhaps because of his insecurity. However, by 1968, he was trying to write more directly and most of the work he brought back from India was less complicated. When a pupil from his old school wrote and asked him to explain the motives behind his songwriting, John replied that the work was done for fun and laughs. "I do it for me first," he said. "Whatever people make of it afterwards is valid, but it doesn't necessarily have to correspond to my thoughts about it, OK? This goes for anyone's 'creations', art, poetry, song etc. The mystery and shit that is built around all forms of art needs smashing anyway."

'Glass Onion' was a playful response by John to those who pored over his work looking for hidden meanings. He started to piece together the song using odd lines and images from some of the most enigmatic Beatles' songs – 'Strawberry Fields Forever', 'There's A Place', 'Within You Without You', 'I Am The Walrus', 'Lady Madonna', 'The Fool On The Hill' and 'Fixing A Hole'. In 'Glass Onion', he jokingly claimed that the walrus, from 'I Am The Walrus', was really Paul. (In some primitive cultures the walrus is a symbol of death and this was taken as confirmation by those who believed that Paul had been killed in a road accident in 1966, to be replaced by a double.) Finally, he came up with four new tantalizing images for his 'literary' fans to pore over – bent-

GLASS ONION
Written:
Lennon/
McCartney
Length: 2' 17"
UK release:
The Beatles album,
November 22,
1968

US release:
The Beatles album,
November 25,
1968

Apple press officer Derek Taylor saw odd flower arrangements in a London restaurant.

back tulips, a glass onion, the Cast-Iron Shore and a dovetail joint. The bent-back tulips, explains former Apple press officer Derek Taylor, was a reference to a particular flower arrangement in Parkes, a fashionable London restaurant in the Sixties.

"You'd be in Parkes sitting around your table and you'd realize that the flowers were actually tulips with their petals bent all the way back, so that you could see the obverse side of the petals and also the stamen. This is what John meant about 'seeing how the other half lives'. He meant seeing how the other half of the flower lives but also, because it was an expensive restaurant, how the other half of society lived."

There were simple explanations for the other perplexing references: the Cast-Iron Shore was Liverpool's own beach (also known as the Cassie); a dovetail joint referred to a wood joint using wedge-shaped tenons and Glass Onion was the name John wanted to use for The Iveys, the band that signed with Apple in July 1968.

The Iveys didn't like the name Glass Onion and, instead, called themselves Badfinger after 'Badfinger Boogie', the original title of 'With A Little Help From My Friends'.

OB-LA-DI OB-LA-DA

Paul first heard the words 'Ob-la-di Ob-la-da' uttered by Nigerian conga player Jimmy Scott, whom he met at the Bag o' Nails club in Soho, London. A flamboyant and unforgettable character in dark glasses and African clothing, Scott was renowned for his catch phrases. His wife Lucrezia says that 'ob la di, ob la da' is a phonetic translation of something that his father would say to him in the Urhobo language used by the Warri people in the mid-West region of Nigeria. "It had a special meaning which he never told anyone," she says. "Even the Beatles didn't know what it meant. When I once asked Paul what it meant he said he thought it meant 'Comme ci, comme ça' but that isn't right. To Jimmy, it was like a philosophy that he took with him through life."

Jimmy Anonmuogharan Scott Emuakpor was born in Sapele, Nigeria, and came to England in the Fifties, where he found work in the jazz clubs of Soho. He played with Georgie Fame and the Blue Flames in the Sixties, backed Stevie Wonder on his 1965 tour of Britain and later formed his own Ob-la-di Ob-la-da Band. He provided music for some of the dance scenes in the Hammer film *She* (1965) that starred Ursula Andress, Peter Cushing and Christopher Lee. Lucrezia says that the phrase was quite well known because in concert he would call out 'Ob la di' and the audience would shout back 'Ob la da' and then Scott would reply 'Life goes on'. The fact that Paul used his catch phrase as the basis of a song ignited controversy. "He got annoyed when I did a song of it because he wanted a cut," Paul told *Playboy* in 1984. "I said 'Come on, Jimmy. It's just an expression. If you'd written the song, you could have had the cut.'"

'Ob-la-di Ob-la-da' has been cited as the first example of white ska; although the phrase was Urhobo, the song Paul created around it and the characters he invented were from Jamaica. When recording the vocals, Paul made a mistake in singing that Desmond, rather than Molly, 'stayed at home and did his pretty face'. The other Beatles liked the slip and so it was kept. Paul loved the song and wanted it to be a single. John always hated it.

Jimmy Scott played congas on the session (July 5, 1968) – the only time he worked with the Beatles. Lucrezia remembers being called in to hear a playback and taking in a headed letter made for the Ob-la-di Ob-la-da Band to show Paul how the phrase was spelt. Later that year, he appeared on the Rolling Stones' *Beggars Banquet* album and in 1969 at the Stones' free concert in Hyde Park. Around this time he was arrested and taken to Brixton prison to await trial on a charge of failing to pay maintenance to his ex-wife. He asked the police to contact the Beatles' office to see if Paul would foot his huge outstanding legal bill. This Paul did, on condition that Scott dropped his case against him over the song.

Scott left England in 1969 and didn't return until 1973 when he immersed himself in the Pyramid Arts project in east London, giving workshops on African music and drumming. In 1983, he joined Bad Manners and was still with them when he died in 1986. "We'd just done this tour of America and he caught pneumonia," remembers Bad Manners' front man Doug Trendle, aka Buster Bloodvessel. "When he got back to Britain he was strip-searched at the airport because he was Nigerian. They left him naked for two hours. The next day he was taken into hospital and he died. Nobody is too sure how old he was because he lied about his age when he got his first British passport. He was supposed to be around 64."

OB-LA-DI OB-LA-DA

Written:	Lennon/McCartney
Length:	3' 08"
UK release:	*The Beatles* album, November 22, 1968
US release:	*The Beatles* album, November 25, 1968

Marmalade saw their version of 'Ob-la-di Ob-la-da' top the UK chart in late 1968.

In July 1986, a concert featuring Bad Manners, Hi Life International, the Panic Brothers, and Lee Perry and the Upsetters was mounted at the Town and Country Club, London, to raise money for the Jimmy Scott Benevolent Fund. He left at least 12 children from two marriages. "Jimmy was essentially a rhythmic, charming, irresistible man with the gift of the gab," Lucrezia wrote in the benefit's programme. "If life was sometimes dull, it shouldn't have been, for his stories of people, of places, of incidents, were an endless stream bubbling with fun."

Paul, who kept in contact with Jimmy, also contributed a quote. "He was a great friend of mine," he wrote. "In the Sixties we used to meet in a lot of clubs and spent many a happy hour chatting until closing time. He had a great positive attitude to life and was a pleasure to work with."

Two British cover versions of 'Ob-la-di Ob-la-da' were recorded and the one by Scottish group Marmalade went to Number 1. The Beatles' version was only released in America, but not until 1976.

WILD HONEY PIE

The shortest and most repetitive of any Beatles' lyric, 'Wild Honey Pie' emerged from a spontaneous singalong in Rishikesh.

"It was just a fragment of an instrumental which we were not sure about," said Paul. "But Pattie Harrison liked it very much, so we decided to leave it on the album."

Coincidentally, Mike Love had recently co-written a Beach Boys' track entitled 'Wild Honey'.

WILD HONEY PIE
Written:
Lennon/
McCartney
Length: 0' 52"
UK release:
The Beatles album,
November 22,
1968
US release:
The Beatles album,
November 25,
1968

The Beatles hanging out in Hyde Park in London in 1967. The identity of the city gent remains unknown.

THE CONTINUING STORY OF BUNGALOW BILL

Bungalow Bill, the song says, 'Went out tiger hunting with his elephant and gun. In case of accidents he always took his mum.' Written by John while in India, it recounts the true story of Richard Cooke III, a young American college graduate, who visited his mother Nancy while she was on the course in Rishikesh.

John described Bungalow Bill as "the all-American bullet-headed Saxon mother's son" and Cooke agrees that it was an accurate description of him when he first met the Beatles. Cooke was over 6ft tall, dressed in white and sporting a crew cut. "The other Beatles were always real nice to me but John was always aloof," he says. "They epitomized the counter culture and I was the classic good American boy and college athlete. There wasn't a whole bunch that we got to connect on."

The tiger-hunt the song refers to took place three hours from Rishikesh. Cooke and his mother travelled by elephant and then hid in a tree on a wooden platform known as a marchand to await the arrival of a tiger.

"Rik sat down and I stood behind him," remembers Nancy. "It wasn't long before I saw this flash of yellow and black. I let out a yell and Rik twirled and shot the tiger right through the ear."

"I was pretty excited that I had shot a tiger," remembers Cooke. "But the Texan who organized the shoot came over to me and said, 'You shot it, but don't say a word. As far as the world is concerned you didn't shoot this tiger.' He wanted to be the one who went back home with the skin and the claws as his trophy."

It was when they arrived at the ashram that Cooke began to feel some remorse, wondering whether the killing of the animal would bring him 'bad karma'. He and his mother had a meeting with Maharishi that was also attended by John and Paul.

"It was a fluke that they happened to be sitting there when I had this conversation with Maharishi," says Cooke. "My mother is a very vocal person and she was talking excitedly about killing the tiger and Maharishi looked pretty aghast that his followers could actually go out and do something like this. It was the only time I ever saw him almost angry."

"Rik told him that he felt bad about it and said that he didn't think he'd ever kill an animal again," recalls Nancy. "Maharishi said – 'You had the desire, Rik, and now you no longer have the desire?' Then John asked, 'Don't you call that slightly life-destructive?' I said, 'It was either the tiger or us. The tiger was jumping right where we were'. That came up in the lyric as 'If looks could kill it would have been us instead of him.'"

Bungalow Bill was an allusion to Buffalo Bill, the performing name of American cowboy showman William Frederick Cody (1846–1917) who was a hero in post-war schoolboy comics. It became 'Bungalow' because all the accommodation in Rishikesh was in bungalows. Ian MacDonald points out in *Revolution In The Head* that the tune appears to be based on 'Stay As Sweet As You Are' which was written by Mack Gordon and Henry Revel and was used in the 1934 film *College Rhythm*.

Cooke knew nothing of 'Bungalow Bill' until he started getting postcards saying 'Hey Bungalow Bill. What did you kill?' from friends who had recognized him in the song. He now divides his time between Hawaii and Oregon and works as a photographer for *National Geographic* magazine. His mother Nancy lives in Beverly Hills, California.

THE CONTINUING STORY OF BUNGALOW BILL

Written:	Lennon/McCartney
Length:	3' 14"
UK release:	*The Beatles* album, November 22, 1968
US release:	*The Beatles* album, November 25, 1968

WHILE MY GUITAR GENTLY WEEPS

WHILE MY GUITAR GENTLY WEEPS
Written:
Harrison
Length: 4' 45''
UK release:
The Beatles album,
November 22,
1968
US release:
The Beatles album,
November 25,
1968

George was reading the I Ching, the Chinese book of changes, and decided to apply its principles of chance to his songwriting. At his parents' Lancashire home, he picked a novel off the shelf with the intention of writing a song based on the first words that he came across. The words were 'gently weeps' and so George began to write.

He started recording in July 1968 but felt that the other Beatles weren't showing sufficient interest in the song. In September, he brought in his friend Eric Clapton to play lead guitar while he played rhythm.

Firmly in his mystical period, George used the I Ching Chinese principle of chance as he wrote 'While My Guitar Gently Weeps'.

HAPPINESS IS
A WARM GUN

For this song, John stitched together three songs that he had started but which didn't seem to be going anywhere. The first was a series of random images picked up from a night of acid tripping with Derek Taylor, Neil Aspinall and Pete Shotton at a house Taylor was renting near Dorking in Surrey. "John said he had written half a song and wanted us to toss out phrases while Neil wrote them down," says Taylor. "First of all, he wanted to know how to describe a girl who was really smart and I remembered a phrase of my father's which was: 'She's not a girl who misses much'. It sounds like faint praise but on Merseyside, in those days, it was actually the best you could get.

"Then I told a story about a chap my wife Joan and I met in the Carrick Bay Hotel on the Isle of Man. It was late one night drinking in the bar and this local fellow who liked meeting holidaymakers and rapping to them suddenly said to us, 'I like wearing moleskin gloves you know. It gives me a little bit of an unusual sensation when I'm out with my girlfriend.' He then said, 'I don't want to go into details.' So we didn't. But that provided the line, 'She's well acquainted with the touch of the velvet hand'. Then there was 'like a lizard on a window pane'. That, to me, was a symbol of very quick movement. Often, when we were living in LA, you'd look up and see tiny little lizards nipping up the window," continues Taylor.

"'The man in the crowd with multi-coloured mirrors on his hobnail boots', was from something I'd seen in a newspaper about a Manchester City soccer fan who had been arrested by the police for having mirrors on the toe caps of his shoes so that he could look up girls' skirts. We thought this was an incredibly complicated and tortuous way of getting a cheap thrill and so that became 'multi-

John often called Yoko 'Mother'; in 'Happiness Is A Warm Gun' she was 'Mother Superior'.

coloured mirrors' and 'hobnail boots' to fit the rhythm. A bit of poetic licence," adds Taylor. "The bit about 'lying with his eyes while his hands were working overtime' came from another thing I'd read where a man wearing a cloak had fake plastic hands, which he would rest on the counter of a shop while underneath the cloak he was busy lifting things and stuffing them in a bag around his waist.

"I don't know where the 'soap impression of his wife' came from but the eating of something and then donating it 'to the National Trust' came from a conversation we'd had about the horrors of walking in public spaces on Merseyside, where you were always coming across the evidence of people having crapped behind bushes and in old air-raid shelters. So to donate what you've eaten to the National Trust (a British organization with responsibilities for upkeeping countryside of great beauty) was what would now be known as 'defecation on common land owned by the National Trust.' When John put it all together, it created a series of layers of images. It was like a whole mess of colour," Taylor concludes.

The second section begins 'I need a fix' and came out of his relationship with Yoko who played a motherly, and some might say superior, role in his life. For most of their relationship he would refer to her as 'Mother'. This was also a time when he was dabbling in heroin, a drug that was later to get a grip on him.

The final section was inspired by something in an American gun magazine that George Martin had pointed out to him. There was a line on the cover reading 'Happiness is a warm gun in your hand…', an obvious play on Peanuts cartoonist Charles Schulz's 1962 book *Happiness is a Warm Puppy*. The apparently bizarre juxtaposition of killing and pleasure stimulated John's imagination at a time. "I thought, what a fantastic thing to say," said John. "A warm gun means that you've just shot something."

The music and vocal delivery of this section emulated 'Angel Baby' by Rosie and the Originals (1960) a track that John loved. *Rolling Stone* writer Jonathan Cott interviewed John on September 18, 1968 and noted that, "John played Rosie and the Originals' version of 'Give Me Love'." This was the B side of 'Angel Baby'. Five days later, John began recording 'Happiness is a Warm Gun'.

On his copy of the lyric sheet John wrote 'dirty old man' by the first section, 'the junkie' by the second and 'the gunman (satire of 50's R + R)' by the third. Sex, drugs and rock 'n' roll!.

HAPPINESS IS A WARM GUN
Written:
Lennon/
McCartney
Length: 2' 43"
UK release:
The Beatles album,
November 22,
1968
US release:
The Beatles album,
November 25,
1968

81

MARTHA MY DEAR

The name Martha came from Paul's two-year-old Old English Sheepdog, but this song is a plea to a girl who has always been the singer's muse: he asks her to remember him because he still believes that they were meant for each other. In January 1968, Paul and Jane Asher had announced that they were going to get married during the year but Paul began dating other girls while Jane was away acting and in July she called off the engagement.

"We still see each other and love each other, but it hasn't worked out," Jane said. "Perhaps we'll be childhood sweethearts and meet again and get married when we're about 70."

The song began as a two-handed piano excercise, something designed to stretch him musically. Explaining the genesis of the song in 1968 he said; "Mainly I come up with a tune and some words come into my head. In this case these happened to be 'Martha my dear'. They don't mean anything. I don't ever try to make serious social comment. You can read anything you like into it but really it's just a song. It's me singing to my dog!"

'Martha My Dear' was recorded in October 1968 – by which time Linda Eastman had become Paul's girl-friend. Jane began a relationship with cartoonist Gerald Scarfe in the early Seventies and they married in 1981.

Paul and Jane Asher went separate ways in 1968 but remained in touch as close friends.

MARTHA MY DEAR
Written:
Lennon/
McCartney
Length: 2' 28"
UK release:
The Beatles album,
November 22,
1968
US release:
The Beatles album,
November 25,
1968

I'M SO TIRED

During the Beatles' stay in Rishikesh, there were two 90-minute lectures each day and much of the rest of the time was taken up with meditating. Students were expected to build up their periods of meditation slowly as their technique improved. One person on the course reportedly claimed to have clocked up a 42-hour session. John found that this life of stillness and inner absorption meant that he couldn't sleep at night and consequently he began feeling tired during the day.

'I'm So Tired', written after three weeks in India, was also about the things he was beginning to miss. The Academy of Meditation was alcohol- and drug- free and John's mind was turning to his beloved cigarettes and the possibility of a drink. Sometimes a friend of his would smuggle some wine in.

Most of all he was missing Yoko Ono. The couple had not yet begun an actual affair because John wasn't sure how to end his marriage. He had briefly entertained the idea of inviting her to India but realized that the complications of having Cynthia and Yoko under the same roof would be too great.

I'M SO TIRED
Written:
Lennon/
McCartney
Length: 2' 03"
UK release:
The Beatles album,
November 22,
1968
US release:
The Beatles album,
November 25,
1968

83

BLACKBIRD

There are a number of stories surrounding the creation of 'Blackbird'. One has it that Paul woke early one morning in Rishikesh to hear a blackbird singing, picked up his guitar to transcribe the bird song and came up with the music. Another suggests that he was inspired by news reports of race riots in America and translated the plight of oppressed racial minorities beginning to flex their muscles into the image of a bird with broken wings struggling to fly.

Paul's step-mother, Angie McCartney, says that it was written for her mother, Edie Stopforth, and that she has a copy of a studio take where Paul says, "This one's for Edie" before recording it. "My mother was staying with Jim and I after a long illness," she says. "During that time Paul visited us and spent some time sitting on mum's bed. She told him that she would often listen to a bird singing at night. Paul eventually took a little tape recorder up to her room and recorded the sound of this bird."

Paul has said that the tune was inspired, not by a blackbird's singing, but by his memory of Bach's Bourrée in E minor (from the lute suite BWV 996) that he had learned as a teenager from a guitar manual. He was partly thinking of the racial situation in America and wrote it as if offering encouragement to the typical black woman facing oppression.

Although written in 1968 it's difficult to pinpoint the exact month since Paul has said that he wrote it not in India but on his Scottish farm. It's likely that he started the music in India, influenced by Donovan, and completed it between his return on March 26 and the demo recordings at George's house late in May. This makes it more likely that the lyric was written in the aftermath of Martin

BLACKBIRD
Written:
Lennon/
McCartney
Length: 2' 18"
UK release:
The Beatles album,
November 22,
1968
US release:
The Beatles album,
November 25,
1968

Luther King's death on April 4. On June 11 he performed it for an Apple promotional film that was being directed by Tony Bramwell.

The use of the term 'blackbird' to refer to people of African origin dates back to the slave trade and was always used pejoratively. In the sixties it was appropriated by the civil rights campaigners and given a positive spin. A civil rights musical, *Fly Blackbird*, with songs by C. Bernard Jackson and James Hatch, opened off-Broadway in 1962 and went on to win an Obie for Best Musical.

In the summer of 1968, Paul serenaded the fans gathered outside his home with an acoustic version of 'Blackbird'. Margo Bird, a former Apple Scruff (the term for the group of fans who used to congregate outside the Apple offices in Savile Row) remembers: "I think he had a young lady round, Francie Schwartz. We'd been hanging around outside and it was obvious she wasn't going to be leaving. He had a music room right at the top of the house and he opened the sash window, sat on the edge and played it to us. It was the early hours of the morning."

Paul often cites 'Blackbird' as evidence that the best of his songs come spontaneously, when words and music tumble out as if they had come into being without conscious effort on his behalf.

The lyric of 'Blackbird' was partly a reflection on the murder of US civil rights activist Martin Luther King.

PIGGIES

George referred to 'Piggies' as "a social comment" although the song did little more than mock the middle-classes by calling them pigs, a Sixties term of derision usually reserved for the police. Pigs were also the animal chosen by George Orwell in *Animal Farm* to represent tyrannical leaders.

The song became notorious in 1971 when it was revealed that Charles Manson, the self-appointed leader of the infamous Manson 'family', had interpreted the words as a warning to the white establishment that they were to get ready for an uprising.

Particularly significant, in Manson's disturbed mind, was the suggestion that the piggies were in need of 'a damn good whacking'. According to witnesses, this was one of Manson's favourite lines, and one that he quoted frequently before his imprisonment for involvement in the murders which many saw as the final dark chapter in the hippie era.

The clue that eventually linked the eight murders – five at the residence of film star Sharon Tate, two at Leno LaBianca's and one at Gary Hinman's – was the painting of the word 'pig', 'pigs' or 'piggy' in the victims' blood. The LaBiancas were even stabbed with knives and forks, apparently because these utensils are mentioned in the last verse.

George was horrified at Manson's misguided interpretation of what he felt was a rather tame song, pointing out that the 'damn good whacking' line had been suggested by his mother when he was looking for something to rhyme with 'backing' and 'lacking'. "It was nothing to do with American policemen or Californian shagnasties," he said.

After murdering eight people in 1971, the Beatles-fixated Charles Manson wrote the word 'Pig' on the walls in their blood.

PIGGIES
Written:
Harrison
Length: 2' 04"
UK release:
The Beatles album,
November 22,
1968
US release:
The Beatles album,
November 25,
1968

ROCKY RACCOON

'Rocky Raccoon' was a musical Western, written by Paul while in India. Set in the mountains of Dakota (probably because of the Doris Day song 'Black Hills Of Dakota' from the movie *Calamity Jane*), it tells the tale of young Rocky whose girl, Nancy Magill, runs off with Dan. Rocky pursues Dan and attempts to shoot him down but is beaten to the draw. Afterwards, Rocky is treated in his hotel room by a doctor stinking of gin. "We were sitting on the roof at Maharishi's just enjoying ourselves when I wrote this one," said Paul. "I started laying the chords and originally the title was 'Rocky Sassoon'. Then me, John and Donovan started making up the words, they came very quickly and eventually it became 'Rocky Raccoon' because it sounded more cowboyish."

The lyric bears more that a passing resemblance to Robert Service's 'The Shooting of Dan McGrew' (1907), a poem that also tells a story of love and revenge with similar-sounding characters. In both works a shooting takes place in a saloon. The femme fatale in Rocky's case is described in the line 'she called herself Lil…but everyone knew her as Nancy'. In Dan McGrew's case the lady is 'known as Lou'.

Apple Scruff Margo Bird heard that the character of the doctor was drawn from real life. "Paul had a quad bike which he came off one day towards the end of 1966. He was a bit stoned at the time and cut his mouth and chipped his tooth," she says. "The doctor who came to treat him was stinking of gin and because he was a bit worse for wear he didn't make a very good job of the stitching. That is why Paul had a nasty lump on his lip for a while and he grew a moustache to cover it."

ROCKY RACCOON

Written:
Lennon/
McCartney

Length: 3' 32"

UK release:
The Beatles album,
November 22,
1968

US release:
The Beatles album,
November 25,
1968

87

DON'T PASS ME BY

'Don't Pass Me By' was Ringo's first complete Beatles' song. Until then, his only contribution to the Beatles' songwriting had been the titles for 'A Hard Day's Night' and 'Tomorrow Never Knows', plus whatever musical contributions he made to 'Flying' and 'What Goes On'.

Asked in December 1967 whether he had aspirations as a songwriter, Ringo replied: "I try. I have a guitar and a piano and play a few chords, but they're all just chinga-lingas. No great tune comes out as far as I'm concerned."

The truth is he'd been trying to get the Beatles to record 'Don't Pass Me By' for years. During an interview for radio in New Zealand on their June 1964 tour of Australasia, Ringo could be heard urging the others to "sing the song I've written, just for a plug". Paul responded by saying: "Ringo has written a song called 'Don't Pass Me By'. A beautiful melody. This is Ringo's first venture into songwriting."

After Paul and John had sung a verse, Ringo was asked more about it: "It was written as a country and western but Paul and John singing it with that blues feeling has knocked me out. Are the Beatles going to record it? I don't know. I don't think so, actually. I keep trying to push it on them every time we make a record."

It was to remain unrecorded for another five years. "Unfortunately, there's never enough time to fit Ringo's song on an album," Paul explained in 1964. "He never finished it."

Ringo spent four years trying to persuade his bandmates to include 'Don't Pass Me By' on a Beatles album.

DON'T PASS ME BY
Written:
Starr
Length: 3' 50"
UK release:
The Beatles album, November 22, 1968
US release:
The Beatles album, November 25, 1968

WHY DON'T WE DO IT IN THE ROAD?

One of the great strengths of the Lennon and McCartney team was that, although they now rarely sat down and created a song from scratch together, they did urge each other on to greater heights in what was increasingly to become solo work.

Sometimes they would try to outdo each other by composing in a style more often associated with the other. *The White Album* contained the sensitive 'Julia' and sentimental 'Goodnight' by John in Paul's style, as well as gritty Lennon-like rock'n'roll numbers like 'Helter Skelter' and 'Why Don't We Do It In The Road?' from Paul. 'Why Don't We Do It In The Road?' upset John because Paul recorded it with Ringo in a separate studio at Abbey Road and Paul's chosen style – a risqué lyric and sparse arrangements – was close to the style he had become associated with.

Paul had the idea for the song while in India when he saw two monkeys copulating in the open. He was struck by the apparently uncomplicated way in which animals mate compared with the rules, rituals and routines of human sex.

"The Beatles have always been a rock group," Paul explained in November 1968. "It's just that we're not completely rock'n'roll. That's why we do 'Ob-La-Di Ob-La-Da' one minute, and this the next. When we played in Hamburg we didn't just play rock'n'roll all evening because we had these fat old businessmen coming in – and thin old businessmen as well – and they would ask us to play a mambo or a samba. I never usually write a song and think: 'Right, now this is going to be about something specific.' It's just that the words happen. I never try to make any serious social point. Just words to go with the music. And you can read anything you like into it."

WHY DON'T WE DO IT IN THE ROAD?
Written:
Lennon/
McCartney
Length: 1' 41"
UK release:
The Beatles album,
November 22,
1968
US release:
The Beatles album,
November 25,
1968

89

I WILL

Paul spent 67 takes getting 'I Will' right on September 16, 1968, with Ringo playing on cymbal and maracas and John tapping the rhythm with a piece of wood. It was the first of Paul's songs to be written about Linda and he was still adding and changing lines as it was being recorded.

Unsurprisingly, there's a sense of anticipation in the lyric, provoked no doubt by the knowledge that Linda and her daughter were arriving in London the very next week. Paul had previously only met Linda in London during the *Sgt Pepper* period and on two subsequent visits to America, but he obviously felt he knew enough about her to be confident in offering her his love 'forever and forever'.

He had started the song in India but being unhappy with the original lyric he stripped it off and started again.

I WILL
Written:
Lennon/
McCartney
Length: 1' 46"
UK release:
The Beatles album,
November 22,
1968
US release:
The Beatles album,
November 25,
1968

'I Will', Paul''s first song about wife-to-be Linda, was written just before she moved to London to live with him.

JULIA

JULIA
Written:
Lennon/
McCartney
Length: 2' 54"
UK release:
The Beatles album,
November 22,
1968
US release:
The Beatles album,
November 25,
1968

Although many of John's songs were shaped by the trauma of losing his mother as a teenager, 'Julia' was the first time he directly introduced his mother into a Beatles' song.

Julia Stanley was born in Liverpool in 1914 and married Frederick Lennon in 1938. John was the only child they had together. By the time John was five, Julia gave birth to another man's child and John was taken into the care of Julia's sister Mimi. His mother was attractive and unconventional. She taught John to play banjo and it was through her that John heard his first Elvis Presley records.

Julia's sudden death in a road accident in 1958 came just when John was becoming close to her again. He'd started using her home in Blomfield Road for band practices with the Quarry Men because Aunt Mimi didn't like loud music in her house.

Although 'Julia' was addressed to his mother, it was also a coded message to his new love, Yoko Ono. The 'ocean child', who John says is calling him, is clearly a reference to Yoko whose name in Japanese means 'child of the ocean'. "It was in India that she began writing to me," John said. "She would write things like 'I am a cloud. Watch for me in the sky.' I would get so excited about her letters."

The first two lines of the song are taken from *Sand And Foam,* a collection of proverbs by the Lebanese mystic, Kahlil Gibran, first published in 1927. Gibran wrote: "Half of what I say is meaningless; but I say it so the other half may reach you." The rest of the song, John said, was finished with help from Yoko herself when they met up back in England because, besides being an artist and film maker, she was a poet who wrote in a minimalist style.

BIRTHDAY

The songs on The Beatles composed in India were guitar-orientated because guitars were the only instruments available at the ashram.

However, 'Birthday' was written in Abbey Road Studios, on September 18, 1968, with Paul thumping out the basic tune on a piano. According to John, Paul had been thinking of 'Happy, Happy Birthday', a 1957 hit in America for the Tuneweavers, but wanted to produce something which sounded contemporary and rock'n'roll. It was also Linda Eastman's 26th birthday in six days' time and Paul knew that she was arriving in London the following week, just in time to celebrate.

Paul went in the studio late in the afternoon and worked out the basic keyboard riff, the start of which was based on the introduction of Rosco Gordon's 'Just A Little Bit' (1960). Later, George, John and Ringo came in and added a backing track. During the evening, the four of them took a break and went round to Paul's house to watch the British television premiere of *The Girl Can't Help It* (1956), which starred Jayne Mansfield and featured music by Fats Domino, Gene Vincent, the Treniers, the Platters, Little Richard and Eddie Cochran.

Perhaps inspired by this dose of early rock'n'roll, the Beatles returned to the studio around 11pm and completed the vocals. Each of the Beatles threw in lines and Yoko Ono and Pattie Harrison helped with the backing. "We just made up the words in the studio," said Paul. "It's one of my favourite tracks on the album because it was instantaneous. It's a good one to dance to."

John's opinion, volunteered 12 years later, was par for the course: "It's a piece of garbage."

Paul wrote 'Birthday' in 1968 to celebrate Linda's 26th birthday.

BIRTHDAY
Written:
Lennon/
McCartney
Length: 2' 42"
UK release:
The Beatles album,
November 22,
1968
US release:
The Beatles album,
November 25,
1968

YER BLUES

'Yer Blues' was the most despairing song John had written to date, representing an anguished cry to Yoko for help. John felt he was at a crossroads in his life: his career as a performing Beatle was nearly over, his manager was dead and now he was contemplating bringing an end to his marriage.

He felt loyalty to Cynthia and yet he knew that in Yoko he'd met his artistic and intellectual match. She was, he later said, the girl he had always dreamed of meeting; the girl he had imagined when he wrote 'Girl'.

During the stay in Rishikesh, John and Cynthia were often separated because of their different meditation routines and it wasn't until the flight back to London from Delhi that John mentioned to Cynthia his indiscretions during their six-year marriage. She was shocked: "I never dreamt that he had been unfaithful to me during our married life. He hadn't revealed anything to me. I knew of course that touring abroad and being surrounded by all the temptations any man could possibly want would have been impossible to resist. But even so my mind just couldn't and wouldn't accept the inevitable. I had never had anything concrete to go on, nothing tell-tale."

John later said that this dilemma had made him feel suicidal. In this song, he jokingly compares himself to 'Mr Jones', the witless central character in Dylan's 'Ballad Of A Thin Man'. Musically, 'Yer Blues' was indicative of the direction he would eventually take with his post-Beatles career.

93

YER BLUES
Written:
Lennon/
McCartney
Length: 4'01"
UK release:
The Beatles album,
November 22,
1968
US release:
The Beatles album,
November 25,
1968

MOTHER NATURE'S SON

Both John and Paul wrote songs after hearing a lecture by the Maharishi about the unity of man and nature, but it was to be Paul's 'Mother Nature's Son' that made the album's final selection.

John's song, 'A Child Of Nature', made similar observations about the sun, sky, wind and mountains but, whereas Paul fictionalized his response by writing in the character of a 'poor young country boy', John wrote about himself 'on the road to Rishikesh'.

A demo of 'A Child Of Nature' was made by John in May 1968, but the Beatles didn't record it. Three years later and with a new set of lyrics it became 'Jealous Guy'.

Paul had always been a lover of the countryside and when he wrote 'Mother Nature's Son' he had in mind a song he had heard when he was younger called 'Nature Boy' (1947) , made popular by Nat 'King' Cole. Although the song was started in India it was completed at his father's house.

Nat 'King' Cole's 1947 hit 'Nature Boy' was in Paul's mind when he composed 'Mother Nature's Son'.

MOTHER NATURE'S SON

Written:	Lennon/McCartney
Length:	2' 48''
UK release:	*The Beatles* album, November 22, 1968
US release:	*The Beatles* album, November 25, 1968

EVERYBODY'S GOT SOMETHING TO HIDE EXCEPT ME AND MY MONKEY

Initially known as 'Come On, Come On', the song was built up from its title. John said it was a clear reference to his relationship with Yoko. "That was just a nice line which I made into a song," he said. "Everybody seemed to be paranoid except for us two, who were in the glow of love...everybody was sort of tense around us."

It wasn't until his return from India that the friendship turned into an affair and Cynthia knew what was happening. Yoko started to attend recording sessions for the new album, much to the annoyance of the other Beatles. The British press also found it difficult to accept Yoko and this irked John and was to play a part in his eventual move to America. "In England, they think I'm someone who has won the pools and gone off with a Japanese Princess," he once said. "In America, they treat her with respect. They treat her as the serious artist she is."

The rapid 'Come on, come on, come on....' chorus sounds similar to what became known as the 'gobble chorus' section of the Fugs' track 'Virgin Forest' that appeared on *The Fugs' Second Album* (1966). Barry Miles, then running the Indica Bookshop, supplied the Beatles with the latest underground releases from America, including work by The Fugs.

95

EVERYBODY'S GOT SOMETHING TO HIDE EXCEPT ME AND MY MONKEY

Written:
Lennon/
McCartney

Length: 2' 24"

UK release:
The Beatles album,
November 22,
1968

US release:
The Beatles album,
November 25,
1968

SEXY SADIE

'Sexy Sadie' appears to be a song about a girl who leads men on, only to make fools of them, but was written about the Maharishi Mahesh Yogi, after John had become disillusioned with him. Knowing that he could never record a potentially libellous song called Maharishi, he titled it 'Sexy Sadie', but on the demo recording of the track he let rip with a string of obscenities directed towards his real quarry.

There were two reasons why the Beatles decided to leave Rishikesh. They had been told that the Maharishi was only after their money and a rumour suggested he had made a sexual advance to a women on the course. It unnerved them and the three Beatles told the guru they were leaving. Pressed to explain their decision, John reportedly said, "Well, if you're so cosmic, you'll know why."

Paul Horn, who remembers them leaving, believes the fall-out was inevitable: "These courses were designed for people who had a solid background in meditation. The Beatles didn't have the experience and I think they were expecting miracles. George was really interested but Ringo wasn't into Eastern philosophy at all. John was and always sceptical about anything until it had been proven to him. Paul was easy-going and could have gone either way.

"The big fuss came because there were some people there who were more interested in the Beatles than learning to meditate and they became hangers-on. One woman was really into the Beatles and started all this crap about the Maharishi making passes at her. There were a lot of rumours, jealousies and triangles going on and she got back at the Beatles through saying this about the Maharishi. The bottom line, though, is that it was time for them to go home. This was just the catalyst."

The band's relationship with the Maharishi did not end well, and John poured his bitterness into 'Sexy Sadie'.

SEXY SADIE
Written:
Lennon/
McCartney
Length: 3' 15''
UK release:
The Beatles album,
November 22,
1968
US release:
The Beatles album,
November 25,
1968

HELTER SKELTER

The concept for 'Helter Skelter' came from a music paper's rave review of a new single by the Who. Paul didn't think the single matched the hyperbole and set himself the challenge of writing something that could legitimately be described in that language.

The single, 'I Can See For Miles', was released in October 1967 and reviewed by Chris Welch in *Melody Maker*. "Forget Happy Jack sitting in sand on the Isle of Man," wrote Welch. "This marathon epic of swearing cymbals and cursing guitars marks the return of the Who as a major freak-out force. Recorded in America, it's a Pete Townshend composition filled with Townshend mystery and menace."

It's impossible to be certain that this was the review, because Paul's description has changed over the years. In 1968, he said the review had said "The group really goes wild with echo and screaming and everything," but 20 years later he claimed it described the Who single as, "the loudest, most raucous rock'n'roll, the dirtiest thing they'd ever done." However, Paul's account of the effect that the review had on him had't changed: "I thought 'That's a pity. I would

HELTER SKELTER

Written:	Lennon/McCartney
Length:	4' 29"
UK release:	*The Beatles* album, November 22, 1968
US release:	*The Beatles* album, November 25, 1968

like to do something like that.' Then I heard it and it was nothing like it. It was straight and sophisticated. So we did this. I like noise."

Despite being described as having 'swearing cymbals' and 'cursing guitars', 'I Can See For Miles' had a discernible melody throughout and could not properly be described as raucous. Paul wanted to write something that really did 'freak people out' and, when the Beatles first recorded 'Helter Skelter' in July 1968, they did it in one take which was almost half an hour long. They returned to it in September 'out of their heads', and produced a shorter version. At the end of it, Ringo can be heard shrieking, "I've got blisters on my fingers."

Most British listeners were aware that a helter skelter was a spiral fairground slide but Charles Manson, who heard the *White Album* in December 1968 thought that the Beatles were warning America of a racial conflict that was 'coming down fast'. In the scenario that Manson had developed, the Beatles were the four angels mentioned in the New Testament book of Revelation who, through their songs, were telling him and his followers to prepare for the coming holocaust by escaping to the desert.

Manson referred to this future uprising as 'Helter Skelter' and it was the daubing of these words in blood at the scene of one of the murders that became another vital clue in the subsequent police investigation. It was because of the song's significance that Vincent Bugliosi, the LA District Attorney who prosecuted at Manson's trial, named his best-selling account of the murders *Helter Skelter*.

Crazed killer Charles Manson felt 'Helter Skelter' was warning America of imminent racial conflict.

LONG LONG LONG

More than any other Beatle, George was inspired to write by hearing other songs. The chords of 'Long Long Long' were suggested to him by Bob Dylan's haunting track 'Sad Eyed Lady Of The Lowlands'. George was fascinated with the movement from D to E minor to A and back to D and wanted to write something which sounded similar. He scribbled the lyric out in the pages of an empty 'week at a glance' diary for 1968 and called it 'It's Been A Long Long Long Time' which then became the working title.

'Long Long Long' sounds like a straightforward love song but, according to George, the 'you' in question here is God. He was the first Beatle to show an interest in Eastern religion and the only one to carry on with it after the others became disenchanted with the Maharishi following their visit to India. George did, however, alter his allegiances, distancing himself from Maharishi and Transcendental Meditation and becoming publicly identified with the International Society for Krishna Consciousness, later producing their Hare Krishna mantra as a hit single.

LONG LONG LONG

Written:	Harrison
Length:	3' 04"
UK release:	*The Beatles* album, November 22, 1968
US release:	*The Beatles* album, November 25, 1968

REVOLUTION

The Summer of Love was followed by the Spring of Revolution. In March 1968, thousands marched on the American Embassy in London's Grosvenor Square to protest against the war in Vietnam. In May, students rioted in Paris. Unlike Mick Jagger, who made an appearance at Grosvenor Square, John surveyed these events from home, keeping in touch through the news media and the underground press. He began work on 'Revolution' while in India and completed it at home when Cynthia was away in Greece. He took it to Paul as a potential single but Paul said the song wasn't commercial enough.

John's refusal to concur with revolutionary politics saw militants condemn his 'betrayal'.

This wasn't the song of a revolutionary but rather the song of someone under pressure from revolutionaries to declare his allegiance. Easily the most politically conscious of the Beatles and unapologetically left-wing in outlook, John had become a target for various Leninist, Trotskyist and Maoist groups, who felt he should lend both moral and financial support to their causes.

'Revolution' was John's reply to these factions, informing them that, while he shared their desire for social change, he believed that the only worthwhile revolution would come about through inner change rather than revolutionary violence. However, he was never absolutely sure of his position, hedging his bets on the slow version of the song released on the album. After admitting that destruction can come with revolution, he sang 'you can count me out/in' obviously unsure of which side of the debate to come down on. On the fast version, recorded six weeks later and released as the B side of 'Hey Jude', he omitted the word 'in'.

The omission provoked much hand-wringing in the underground press. The American magazine *Ramparts* called it a 'betrayal' and the

New Left Review: "a lamentable petty bourgeois cry of fear". *Time* magazine, on the other hand, devoted a whole article to the song which it said, "criticized radical activists the world over".

The nature of John's dilemma was revealed in an exchange of letters published in a Keele University magazine. In an open letter, student John Hoyland said of 'Revolution', "That record was no more revolutionary than *Mrs Dale's Diary* (a BBC radio soap). In order to change the world, we've got to understand what's wrong with the world. And then – destroy it. Ruthlessly. This is not cruelty or madness. It is one of the most passionate forms of love. Because what we're fighting is suffering, oppression, humiliation – the immense toll of unhappiness caused by capitalism. And any 'love' which does not pit itself against these things is sloppy and irrelevant. There is no such thing as a polite revolution."

In his reply, John wrote: "I don't remember saying that 'Revolution' was revolutionary. Fuck Mrs Dale. Listen to all three versions of 'Revolution' – 1, 2 and 9 and then try again, dear John (Hoyland). You say 'in order to change the world, we've got to understand what's wrong with the world and then destroy it. Ruthlessly'. You're obviously on a destruction kick. I'll tell you what's wrong with it – people. So, do you want to destroy them? Ruthlessly? Until you/we change your/our heads – there's no chance. Tell me one successful revolution. Who fucked up communism, Christianity, capitalism, Buddhism etc? Sick heads, and nothing else. Do you think all the enemy wear capitalist badges so that you can shoot them? It's a bit naive, John. You seem to think it's just a class war."

Interviewed later by journalists from the magazine, John (Lennon) said: "All I'm saying is I think you should do it by changing people's heads, and they're saying we should smash the system. Now the system-smashing scene has been going on forever. What's it done? The Irish did it, the Russians did it and the French did it and where has it got them? It's got them nowhere. It's the same old game. Who's going to run this smashing up? Who's going to take over? It'll be the biggest smashers. They'll be the ones to get in first and, like in Russia, they'll be the ones to take over. I don't know what the answer is but I think it's down to people."

It was a position John was to hold to. In 1980, he said that 'Revolution' still stood as an expression of his politics. "Count me out if it's for violence. Don't expect me on the barricades unless it's with flowers."

REVOLUTION

Written:
Lennon/
McCartney

Length: 4' 15"

UK single release:
August 30, 1968
as B-side to
'Hey Jude'

US single release:
August 26, 1968
as B-side to
'Hey Jude'

HONEY PIE

'Honey Pie' was a tribute to Jim McCartney from his son. "My dad's always played fruity old songs like this, and I like them," Paul said. "I would have liked to have been a writer in the Twenties because I like the top hat and tails thing."

Just as he believed 'Helter Skelter' was written for him personally, Charles Manson found further instructions in 'Honey Pie'. After all, it was addressed to people in the USA, inviting them to display the magic of their 'Hollywood song'? Manson lived near Los Angeles. What could be clearer?

SAVOY TRUFFLE

George had been friendly with Eric Clapton since meeting him in April 1966 and 'Savoy Truffle' was a playful song about Clapton's love of chocolate. This habit contributed to Clapton's tooth decay and George was warning him that one more soft-centred chocolate and he'd have to have his teeth pulled out.

The song's lyric is made up of the exotic names then given to individual chocolates in Mackintosh's Good News assortment such as Creme Tangerine, Montelimar, Ginger Sling and Coffee Dessert. Savoy Truffle was another authentic name, whereas Cherry Cream and Coconut Fudge were invented to fit the song.

Derek Taylor helped with the middle eight by suggesting the title of a film he'd just seen called *You Are What You Eat* which was made by two American friends, Alan Pariser and Barry Feinstein. It didn't scan properly so George changed it to 'you know that what you eat you are'.

HONEY PIE
Written:
Lennon/McCartney
Length: 2' 41"
UK release:
The Beatles album,
November 22, 1968
US release:
The Beatles album,
November 25, 1968

SAVOY TRUFFLE
Written: Harrison
Length: 2' 54"
UK release:
The Beatles album,
November 22, 1968
US release:
The Beatles album,
November 25, 1968

CRY BABY CRY

CRY BABY CRY
Written:
Lennon/
McCartney
Length: 3'01"
UK release:
The Beatles album,
November 22,
1968
US release:
The Beatles album,
November 25,
1968

In 1968, as Hunter Davies was finishing his band biography, John told him: "I've got another (song) here, a few words, I think I got them from an advert: 'Cry baby cry, Make your mother buy'. I've been playing it over on the piano. I've let it go now. It'll come back if I really want it." The lines came back to him while he was in India where Donovan remembers him working on it. "I think the eventual imagery was suggested by my own songs of fairy tales. We had become very close in exchanging musical vibes."

Partly based on the nursery rhyme 'Sing A Song Of Sixpence' and, via the advert, partly on the playground taunt 'Cry, baby, cry,/ Stick a finger in your eye/ And tell your mother it wasn't I', the song includes John's own creations the Duchess of Kirkaldy and the King of Marigold. Kirkaldy is in Fife, Scotland, and was where John used to stop off on his way to Durness for family holidays as a boy.

John's keen embrace of
psychedelia extended
to his Rolls-Royce.

REVOLUTION 9

'Revolution 9' was neither a Lennon and McCartney song nor a Beatles' recording but an eight minute, 15 second-long amalgamation of taped sounds which John and Yoko mixed together.

The album track of 'Revolution' originally clocked in at over 10 minutes; more than half of it consisting of John and Yoko screaming and moaning over a range of discordant sounds, created to simulate the rumblings of a revolution. Subsequently, they decided to clip the chaotic section and use it as the basis of another track, which turned into 'Revolution 9'.

At this point, home-made tapes of crowd disturbances were brought in and other sound effects were found in EMI's library. Due to the lack of sophisticated multi-track recording, all three Abbey Road studios had to be commandeered, with machines being specially linked together and tape loops held in place with pencils. John operated the faders to create a live mix.

With so many overlapping sounds, it is almost impossible to identify all the individual noises and spoken comments. Mark

REVOLUTION 9

Written:	Lennon/McCartney
Length:	8' 22"
UK release:	*The Beatles* album, November 22, 1968
US release:	*The Beatles* album, November 25, 1968

The sonic collage of 'Revolution 9' included a recording of John and Yoko screaming the word 'right'.

Lewisohn, who studied the original four-track recording, divided these into: a choir; backwards violins; a backwards symphony; an orchestral overdub from 'A Day In The Life'; banging glasses; applause; opera; backwards mellotron; humming; spoken phrases by John and George and a cassette tape of Yoko and John screaming the word 'right' from 'Revolution'.

The most memorable tape, (which supplied part of the title), was the sonorous voice intoning 'Number Nine, Number Nine'. This was apparently discovered on a library tape, which may have formed part of a taped examination question for students of the Royal Academy of Music.

Once again, Charles Manson thought that John was speaking personally to him through the hubbub, taking the number 9 as a reference to Revelation chapter 9 with its vision of the coming apocalypse. Manson thought John was shouting 'rise', rather than 'right', and interpreted it as an incitement to the black community to rise against the white middle class. 'Rise' became one of Manson's key phrases and was found painted in blood at one of the murder scenes.

Paul was in America when 'Revolution 9' was put together and was disappointed at its inclusion on *The Beatles*, particularly as he had been making sound collages at home since 1966 and realized that John would now be seen as the innovator.

GOOD NIGHT

'Good Night' is certainly the most schmaltzy song ever written by John. If it had been one of Paul's songs, John would probably have dismissed it as "garbage" but his final comment was only that it was possibly "over-lush".

John wrote it, he said, for Julian as a bedtime song just as, 12 years later, he would write 'Beautiful Boy' for his second son, Sean. The melody appears to have been 'inspired' by Cole Porter's 'True Love' (1956) song from the musical *High Society* that became a hit for Bing Crosby and Grace Kelly.

Julian wasn't aware that John had written the song for him until he was interviewed for this book. This was probably due to the fact that his parents split up within a few weeks of its composition.

GOOD NIGHT

Written:	Lennon/McCartney
Length:	3' 11"
UK release:	*The Beatles* album, November 22, 1968
US release:	*The Beatles* album, November 25, 1968

DON'T LET ME DOWN

DON'T LET ME DOWN
UK single release:
April 11, 1969, as B-side of 'Get Back'
US single release:
May 5, 1969, as B-side of 'Get Back'

John had always expressed fears of being let down by those he had put his trust in. 'If I Fell' was the template for a number of songs in which he confessed his need for love and his anxiety over being rejected.

Written about Yoko and released as the B side of 'Get Back' in April 1969, this same old worry was expressed as an agonizing cry having found someone who loved him more than anyone had ever done before. Influenced by Yoko's minimalist approach to art, he has cut out all embellishments, reducing his perennial plea to the form of an urgent telegram.

John and Yoko in 1968 leaving Marylebone Court, where he had admitted possession of cannabis resin.

LET IT BE

Committed to completing a final movie for United Artists, but with no inclination of emulating *Help* or *A Hard Day's Write*, the Beatles fulfilled their contract with *Let It Be*, an 80-minute colour documentary of the group rehearsing at Twickenham Film Studios, recording at Apple Studios and playing live on the roof of the Apple office in London. These three strands were filmed in January 1969 but the film wasn't premiered until May 1970, when a boxed album and book set was prepared for the release. The album wasn't available separately until November 1970.

The plan had been to make an album called *Get Back* and to film the recording process for a television documentary. There was a possibility of including a live show and a number of venues were considered – the Roundhouse in London, Liverpool Cathedral, the QE2, Tripoli, Tahiti and a Roman amphitheatre in Tunisia.

The film and album that evolved involved compromises. Instead of being a document of musical creativity, *Let It Be* became a record of musical disintegration. To get the album finished, Paul assumed control, pushing and prodding where necessary, while John and George sulked, openly displaying their resentment.

Rows over the album contributed to the group's final break-up. The American Allen Klein, now acting as their manager, wasn't happy with the quality of the tapes which engineer Glyn Johns had edited down, and so he brought in a fellow American, the producer Phil Spector, to beef up the production. When Paul heard what Spector had done to 'The Long And Winding Road', he requested that it be restored to its original form. After this request was ignored, Paul announced his departure from the Beatles.

The Beatles pictured with Yoko listening to *Let It Be*. At one time they all stood together. Now they sat apart, barely able to conceal their differences.

The *Let It Be* album was scrappy. Because it was the last album released, it's often assumed it was the last album recorded. But, after the squabbling that characterized *Let It Be*, the Beatles went on to record *Abbey Road*, an album which George Martin still ranks as his favourite.

By the time *Let It Be* was released the Beatles had disbanded. Paul had already released his first solo album, although it wasn't until December 1970 that their union was officially dissolved following Paul's lawsuit. *Let It Be* reached the top of the British and American album charts after its release in May 1970. The advance orders of almost four million in the US were the largest for any album ever. In 2003 the album was re-released with Spector's contributions wiped off and titled *Let It Be… Naked*. The running order was re-shuffled, 'I've Got A Feeling' (originally the B side to 'Get Back') was added and 'Dig It' and 'Maggie Mae' were left off. The plan was to restore the album to what the four Beatles had originally intended.

TWO OF US

Performed in the documentary by John and Paul on acoustic guitars, 'Two Of Us' sounds like a song about their Liverpool teenage years together – burning matches, lifting latches and going home to play more music together. But the 'two of us' were not Paul and John but Paul and Linda. One of the most attractive things to Paul about his new girlfriend was her unpretentious 'hang-loose' approach to everything. In a life restricted by schedules and contractual obligations, he relished being with someone who seemed consistently laid-back, someone with whom he could forget he was a Beatle.

Soon after they met in London during the autumn of 1968, Linda taught Paul the joys of getting completely lost. She would drive him out of the city with no destination in mind and with the sole intention of ending up miles from anywhere. To a Beatle, who was constantly told where and when he was needed this was an exhilarating return to freedom. "As a kid I loved getting lost," explains Linda. "I would say to my father – let's get lost. But you could never seem to be able to get really lost. All signs would eventually lead back to New York or wherever we were staying! Then, when I moved to England to be with Paul, we would put Martha in the back of the car and drive out of London. As soon as we were on the open road I'd say 'Let's get lost' and we'd keep driving without looking at any signs. Hence the line in the song 'two of us going nowhere'.

"Paul wrote 'Two Of Us' on one of those days out," Linda explains. "It's about us. We just pulled off in a wood somewhere and parked the car. I went off walking while Paul sat in the car and started writing. He also mentions the postcards because we used to send a lot of postcards to each other."

Loving Linda's laid-back nature, Paul wrote 'Two Of Us' about their relationship.

TWO OF US
Written:
Lennon/
McCartney
Length:
3' 36"
UK release:
Let It Be album,
May 8, 1970
US release:
Let It Be album,
May 18, 1970

DIG A PONY

'Dig A Pony' was largely composed in the studio and the words make very little sense. At one point it was called 'Con A Lowry' (possibly a reference to a make of organ used in the studio) but John changed it to 'Dig A Pony', "because 'I con a Lowry' didn't sing well... It's got to be d's and p's, you know."

Similarly, the line 'I do a road hog' started as 'I dig a skylight' and then became 'I did a groundhog'. "It had to be rougher," John argued. "I don't care if skylight was prettier." The chorus was taken from a separate song of John's written about Yoko called 'All I Want Is You'. The original song listing for the album used this title rather than 'Dig A Pony'.

In January 1969 when the song was recorded, John explained the secret of its composition, "I just make it up as I go along". In September 1980, he laconically concluded, "(just) another piece of garbage".

DIG A PONY

Written:	Lennon/McCartney
Length:	3' 54"
UK release:	*Let It Be* album, May 8, 1970
US release:	*Let It Be* album, May 18, 1970

ACROSS THE UNIVERSE

The oldest song on the *Let It Be* album, 'Across The Universe' was recorded in February 1968 and first featured on a charity album for the World Wildlife Fund in December 1969.

A song about writing songs, or at least about the mysteries of the creative process, John was often to refer to it as one of his favourite Beatles' songs because of the purity of the lyric. The words had come to him while in bed at Kenwood. He had been arguing with Cynthia and, as he lay there trying to sleep, the phrase 'pools of sorrow, waves of joy' came to him and wouldn't leave until he got up and started writing the words down. "It drove me out of bed," John said. "I didn't want to write it. I was just slightly irritable and I couldn't go to sleep."

Written after having met the Maharishi Mahesh Yogi in England but before studying with him in India the chorus mentions Guru Dev, who was Maharishi's guru. John wanted this to be the single that the Beatles put out while they were away in India but it lost out to 'Lady Madonna'. David Bowie later recorded a cover version for his *Young Americans* album (1975) on which John played guitar.

David Bowie recorded a cover of 'Across The Universe' for his *Young Americans* album. John helped out on guitar.

ACROSS THE UNIVERSE

Written:	Lennon/McCartney
Length:	3' 48"
UK release:	*Let It Be* album, May 8, 1970
US release:	*Let It Be* album, May 18, 1970

I ME MINE

As George became more deeply involved in Eastern thought, he tried to reconcile his position as a rock star with the religious demands of relinquishing his ego in order to attain enlightenment.

It was his belief that it is our preoccupation with our individual egos – what 'I' want, what belongs to 'me', what's 'mine' – that prevents us from being absorbed into the universal consciousness, where there is no duality and no ego. "There is nothing that isn't part of the complete whole," George said. "When the little 'i' merges into the big 'I', then you are really smiling!"

The waltz tune of 'I Me Mine' was inspired by Johann Strauss II's 'Kaiserwalzer', a 60-second extract of which had been used as background music on a BBC2 TV documentary *Europa: The Titled and the Unentitled* the evening before. The version was by the Vienna Philharmonic Orchestra conducted by Willi Boskovsky. George had seen the programme and developed a tune from what he remembered.

I ME MINE

Written:	Harrison
Length:	2' 25"
UK release:	*Let It Be* album, May 8, 1970
US release:	*Let It Be* album, May 18, 1970

DIG IT

Credited to all four Beatles, 'Dig It' started as a fledgling song by John called 'Can You Dig It' which consisted of variations of the title being sung over a riff.

The version released on *Let It Be* was an excerpt from a much longer jam in which all the Beatles made up lines on the spot, hence the shared composer credit.

There was a lot of time spent hanging around reading newspapers when they recorded which might account for the references to the FBI and CIA. Transcripts of studio conversations reveal George talking about blues guitarist B B King and distinguishing him from fellow blues man Freddie King. Matt Busby was the heroic manager of Manchester United, one of England's most popular and successful football teams. Busby would have been in the news because twelve days before this recording he had announced his retirement after 24 years with the club.

DIG IT
Written:
Harrison/Lennon/
McCartney/Starr
Length: 0' 50"
UK release:
Let It Be album,
May 8, 1970
US release:
Let It Be album,
May 18, 1970

George was keen to tell his blues men apart during the recording session for 'Dig It'.

LET IT BE

LET IT BE
Written:
Lennon/
McCartney
Length: 4' 03"
UK single release:
March 6, 1970
UK chart
position: 2
US single release:
March 11, 1970
US chart
position: 1

Released as a single in March 1970, 'Let It Be' sounded as if it had been recorded as the Beatles' swansong yet it dated from January 1969. No one had any idea that it was going to be the last single.

Paul had written 'Let It Be' out of his general feelings of despair, as the Beatles began to fall apart at the seams. The documentary had started out as a record of a rehearsal followed by a live performance, but it was to become a record of the group's death throes.

By now, John preferred to spend his time with Yoko whose presence around the studio was not welcomed by everyone. George had already quit the group once and was discouraged at the way his songs were being instantly rejected. Even Ringo had taken off for a short holiday during the recording of *The White Album* when the atmosphere got really bad.

Paul was clearly trying to take over the role of leader because he felt that without organization and discipline nothing would be achieved. "I think we've been very negative since Mr Epstein passed away," Paul can be heard saying in the film. "We haven't been positive. That's why all of us in turn have been sick of the group. There's nothing positive in it. It's a bit of a drag. The only way for it not to be a bit of a drag is for the four of us to think – should we make it positive or should we forget it?"

Although Paul's role may have been necessary, it didn't make him popular. The others began to resent his role as organiser. 'Let It Be' was written by Paul as a response to all this pressure: "I wrote it when all those business problems started to get me down," he said. "I really was passing through my 'hour of darkness' and writing the song was my way of exorcizing the ghosts."

115

I'VE GOT A FEELING

'I've Got A Feeling' was again two unfinished songs strung together, this time Paul's 'I've Got A Feeling' and John's 'Everybody's Had A Hard Year'. Paul's song, optimistic as ever, was presumably written for Linda just to tell her that she was the girl he'd always been looking for. John's song was a litany where every line began with the word 'everybody'.

John had indeed been through a hard year. His marriage to Cynthia had ended, he was separated from his son Julian, Yoko had suffered a miscarriage, he had been arrested on a charge of drug possession and he reckoned his personal fortune had dwindled to about £50,000.

During the filming of *Let It Be*, John ran through 'Everybody Had A Hard Year' and said, somewhat tongue in cheek, that it was something he had started writing the night before. If this were true, it would date the song's origin to January 1969, but there is BBC film of him shot in December 1968, where he is singing the song with an acoustic guitar in the garden of his Ascot home.

I'VE GOT A FEELING

Written:	Lennon/McCartney
Length:	3' 37"
UK release:	*Let It Be* album, May 8, 1970
US release:	*Let It Be* album, May 18, 1970

THE LONG AND WINDING ROAD

THE LONG AND WINDING ROAD
Written:
Lennon/
McCartney
Length: 3' 37''
UK release:
Let It Be album,
May 8, 1970
US release:
Let It Be album,
May 18, 1970

Like 'Yesterday', 'The Long And Winding Road' evokes loss without describing any specific situation. The images of wind and rain suggest feelings of being abandoned in the wilderness, while the long and winding road leading to 'her door' is the sign of hope.

The imagery actually comes from Paul's experience of staying at High Park, his farm in Scotland, which is exposed to high winds and frequently lashed with rain. The long and winding road itself is the B842, over twenty five miles of twists and turns which runs down the east coast of Kintyre into Campbeltown, the nearest town to the farm.

Paul has said that he had the voice of Ray Charles in mind when he wrote it and that this influenced the use of jazzy chords. The road he envisaged as an endless road because the song is about what is eventually unattainable.

It was released as a single in America in May 1970 and reached the Number 1 spot.

117

Paul was thinking of Ray Charles when he wrote 'The Long And Winding Road'.

ONE AFTER 909

'One After 909' could well be the oldest Lennon and McCartney song ever to be recorded by the Beatles. It was one of 'over a hundred songs' which they often talked about having written before recording 'Love Me Do' and goes back to that time together at Forthlin Road.

The Beatles first recorded 'One After 909' in March 1963 during the same session which produced 'From Me To You' but George Martin was so unimpressed with it that it had never been released. It was an attempt by John, in 1957, to write an American railroad song, after skiffle hits such as 'Last Train To San Fernando' by Johnny Duncan, 'Cumberland Gap' and 'Rock Island Line' by Lonnie Donegan and 'Freight Train' by the Chas McDevitt Skiffle Group.

"We used to sag (play truant) off school, go back to my house and the two of us would write," Paul recalled. "There are a lot of songs from back then that we've never reckoned on because they're all very unsophisticated songs...We hated the words to 'One After 909'."

When they came to play around with it during the sessions there was chat between John and Paul where they mentioned how they had originally dropped it because they'd always considered the lyric illogical and unfinished.

ONE AFTER 909
Written:
Lennon/
McCartney
Length: 2' 55"
UK release:
Let It Be album,
May 8, 1970
US release:
Let It Be album,
May 18, 1970

FOR YOU BLUE

FOR YOU BLUE
Written:
Harrison
Length: 2' 32"
UK release:
Let It Be album,
May 8, 1970
US release:
Let It Be album,
May 18, 1970

Completed in six takes, 'For You Blue' was known as 'George's Blues' and on George's original lyric sheet as 'For You Blues' but became 'For You Blue' on the album.

George was always the Beatle most keen to develop his musical skills and it was through this that he developed close friendships with musicians as diverse as Ravi Shankar and Eric Clapton. It also led him to constantly experiment with different tunings, instruments and styles of playing.

Written for Pattie, 'For You Blue' was an exercise in writing a traditional blues song. George's only comment on it was to say: "It's a simple 12-bar song following all the normal 12-bar principles except that it's happy-go-lucky!"

George wrote his trad blues song 'For You Blue' for Pattie Boyd.

GET BACK

Paul said that he'd originally written 'Get Back' "as a political song" and surviving demos show that he was planning a satire on the attitudes of those who felt that immigrants to Britain should be repatriated. It was to be sung from the point of view of someone who didn't 'dig no Pakistanis taking all the people's jobs' and so was urging them to 'get back' to where they came from, its satirical intentions could easily have been misconstrued.

Years later, Paul was still having to field questions from journalists who'd heard bootleg editions of this version and who wondered if he'd gone through a racist period. "(The verses) were not racist at all," he said. "If there was any group that was not racist, it was the Beatles. All our favourite people were always black."

By the time it was recorded, 'Get Back' had been transformed into a song about Jojo from Tucson, Arizona, (Linda Eastman lived for a while in Tucson) and Loretta Martin who 'thought she was a woman, But she was another man'. No story was developed and the original 'Get back' chorus was retained. Because it was a rock'n'roll song, 'Get Back' was taken to refer to a return to musical roots and Apple's newspaper advert which bore the slogan 'The Beatles as nature intended' appeared to confirm this notion. "'Get Back' is the Beatles' new single," ran the copy. "It's the first Beatles' record which is as live as can be, in this electronic age. There's no electronic watchamacallit. 'Get Back' is a pure spring-time rock number."

It went on to quote Paul saying, "We were sitting in the studio and we made it up out of thin air…we started to write words there and then…when we finished it, we recorded it at Apple Studios and made it into a song to rollercoast by."

Paul originally penned 'Get Back' as a satire aimed at racists.

GET BACK
Written:
Lennon/
McCartney
Length: 3'07"
UK single release:
April 11, 1969
**UK chart
position:** 1
US single release:
May 5, 1969
**US chart
position:** 1

THE BALLAD OF JOHN AND YOKO

'The Ballad Of John And Yoko' – in which John related the details of his marriage to Yoko in Gibraltar and their subsequent 'honeymoon' – was recorded in mid-April and released before the end of May. Paul helped with the final verse. The song portrayed the couple as victims about to be 'crucified': the two are turned back at Southampton docks, can't get a wedding licence in France, then they're misunderstood as they lie in bed 'for peace' and laughed at when they sit in a bag.

Something John failed to mention was the fact that they were turned back at Southampton dock not because of his notoriety but because they were trying to travel to France without passports. The plane they 'finally made' into Paris was not a scheduled airliner but an executive jet which John impatiently asked for when he realized that it was impossible to get married on a cross-Channel ferry.

John's decision to get married appeared to have been made suddenly on March 14, 1969, when he and Yoko were being driven down to Poole in Dorset to visit his Aunt Mimi. This was two days after Paul's registry office wedding to Linda. John asked his chauffeur Les Anthony to go on into Southampton and enquire about the possibility of their being married at sea. When this was found to be impossible, John decided to go to Paris and instructed his office to come up with a way of arranging a quiet wedding there. Peter Brown discovered that this couldn't be organized at short notice but that they could marry in Gibraltar because it was a British protectorate and John was a British citizen.

In the end, the couple flew by private plane to Gibraltar on March 20, and went straight to the British Consulate where the registrar, Cecil

THE BALLAD OF JOHN AND YOKO
Written:
Lennon/ McCartney
Length: 2' 55''
UK single release:
May 30, 1969
UK chart position: 1
US single release:
June 4, 1969
US chart position: 8

[2]

Wheeler, conducted a ten-minute marriage ceremony. They were on the ground for less than an hour before taking off for Amsterdam where they had booked the Presidential Suite at the Hilton. Their stay in Amsterdam was to be an extraordinary 'honeymoon'. Instead of requiring the usual privacy, they invited the world's press to invade their bedroom daily between 10:00 am and 10:00 pm during which time, they said, they would be staying in bed for peace.

Not unnaturally, the world's press hoped that John and Yoko might be intending to consummate their marriage in public. After all, they'd exposed their naked bodies on the cover of their album *Two Virgins* and had recorded the heartbeat of the child that Yoko later miscarried. There seemed to be no area of their lives that they weren't willing to turn into performance art.

To the journalists' frustration, the sight that greeted them in suite 902 was of John and Yoko in neatly pressed pyjamas sitting bolt upright in bed doing nothing more than talking about 'peace'. It was the perfect deal. The media had an insatiable appetite for articles about the Beatles and John would do almost anything to put over his message about peace. The Amsterdam 'Bed In' meant that all parties went away satisfied.

For seven days, they lay there holding court while a stream of media people sat and asked serious questions. The coverage was incredible. They did live interviews with American radio stations, made a sixty-minute documentary for themselves and saw their faces appear on the front pages of newspapers world-wide. "Yoko and I are quite willing to be the world's clowns, if by doing it we do some good," said John. "For reasons known only to themselves people do print what I say. And I'm saying peace. We're not pointing a finger at anybody. There are no good guys and bad guys. The struggle is in the mind. We must bury our own monsters and stop condemning people. We are all Christ and all Hitler. We want Christ to win. We're trying to make Christ's message contemporary. What would he have done if he had advertisements, records, films, TV and newspapers? Christ made miracles to tell his message. Well, the miracle today is communications, so let's use it."

From Amsterdam, they went to Vienna where they stopped overnight at the Hotel Sacher and ate some of its famous Sacher Torte (a rich chocolate cake) before watching the television premiere of their film *Rape*.

On April 1, they arrived back in London and gave a press conference at the airport. John expected a hostile reception because Yoko (a foreign divorcée, no less) was not considered the ideal partner for a British Beatle. To his surprise, the welcome was warm.

'The Ballad Of John And Yoko' was recorded by Paul and John with Paul playing bass, piano, maracas and drums, while John played lead and acoustic guitars and sang the vocals.

123

John and Yoko's famous 'Bed In' for peace saw them conduct a week's worth of interviews between the sheets.

OLD BROWN SHOE

'Old Brown Shoe' was one of three songs which George made a demo of at Abbey Road on February 25, 1969. The other two were 'Something', a future Beatles' single, and 'All Things Must Pass', the title track of his first solo album in 1970.

George poured his cosmic worldview into 'Old Brown Shoe'.

The lyric had its origins in George's religious view that we must free ourselves from the reality of the material world as it is illusory. Once absorbed into the divine consciousness, there would be no right versus wrong, body versus soul, spirit versus matter. Rather like Paul had done with 'Hello Goodbye', George's words were a game based on opposites. It wasn't a song which told much of a story and the intriguing title was pinched from a line about stepping out of 'this old brown shoe'. (George always had a problem coming up with titles.)

The main inspiration was musical. George had been messing around on a piano one day and hit on a chord sequence he liked. Words were added later.

Recorded two months after being demoed, 'Old Brown Shoe' became the B side of 'The Ballad Of John And Yoko'. Much later it was used as a track on the compilation albums *Hey Jude* and *The Beatles 1967–1970*.

OLD BROWN SHOE
Written: Harrison
Length: 3' 16"
UK single release: May 30, 1969 as B-side of 'The Ballad of John and Yoko'
US single release: June 4, 1969 as B-side of 'The Ballad of John and Yoko'

YOU KNOW MY NAME

Released as the B side of 'Let It Be', 'You Know My Name' was the strangest single ever released by the Beatles and remains one of their least-known songs.

It had first been recorded shortly after the completion of *Sgt Pepper*, after John arrived at Abbey Road wanting to record a song called 'You Know My Name, Look Up The Number'. When Paul asked to see the lyric, John told him that was the lyric. He wanted it repeated in the style of the Four Tops' 'Reach Out, I'll Be There' until it sounded like a mantra. The line was a variation on a slogan John had noticed on the front cover of the Post Office's London telephone directory for 1967 which read; 'You have their NAME? Look up their NUMBER.'

For three days in May and June 1967, the Beatles worked on the song but then abandoned it until April 1969 when the track was taken out for reworking. Although John's original idea of repeating the title phrase was adhered to, the song was transformed from a mantra into what sounded like a karaoke night in Hell, organized by the Goons or the Bonzo Dog Doo Dah Band.

The only departure from the scripted words came when John twice asked for a big hand for 'Denis O'Bell', a reference to the Irish-born film producer Denis O'Dell who had been Associate Producer on *A Hard Day's Night* and who had become director of Apple Films and Apple Publicity.

None of the Beatles told O'Dell that they had referred to him in the song and so it came as a shock to him when he started receiving anonymous telephone calls at his home in St George's Square, Pimlico.

YOU KNOW MY NAME
Written:
Lennon/
McCartney
Length: 4' 19"
UK single release:
March 6, 1970,
as B-side of 'Let
It Be'
US single release:
March 11, 1970,
as B-side of 'Let
It Be'

ABBEY ROAD

Seven years on from their first recordings at the Abbey Road Studios, the Beatles returned for what proved to be their final sessions. Back in June 1962, they were wide-eyed provincial lads keen to make their mark on the music business. By July 1969, they had become world-weary sophisticates, their lives blighted by struggles over power and money.

The songs on *Abbey Road* reflected their frustrations. They're about legal negotiations, unpaid debts, being ripped off, bad karma and generally bearing the weight of the world on your shoulders. There was even a mock-jolly song about a silver hammer (namely Maxwell's) that is waiting to come down hard on you just when things are starting to get better.

Despite this mood – or perhaps because of it – *Abbey Road* was an outstandingly inventive farewell offering. It features two of George's best songs, 'Here Comes The Sun' and 'Something'; a stand-out track by John, 'Come Together', and a fascinating medley of half-finished songs skilfully woven together by Paul.

George Martin remembered that after *Let It Be*, Paul came to him and asked him to produce a Beatles' album with the kind of feeling they used to generate together. Martin agreed to help out if the Beatles were prepared to give him their co-operation. "That's how we made *Abbey Road*. It wasn't quite like the old days because they were still working on their old songs and they would bring in the other people to work as kind of musicians for them rather than being a team."

In Britain, *Abbey Road* was released in September 1969 and stayed at Number 1 for 18 weeks. In America, it was released in October and was at Number 1 for 11 weeks.

COME TOGETHER

'Come Together' started life as a campaign song for Timothy Leary , when he decided in 1969 that he was going to run as governor of California against America's future president Ronald Reagan.

Abbey Road saw the band vent feelings of frustration and ennui but was still a hugely inventive album.

Leary and his wife Rosemary were invited up to Montreal, where John and Yoko were between the sheets for another major 'bed in' on the 19th floor of the Queen Elizabeth Hotel. They arrived on June 1, 1969, and were promptly roped into singing on the chorus of 'Give Peace A Chance', which was recorded in the hotel bedroom. Leary and his wife were rewarded for their participation by having their names included in the lyric.

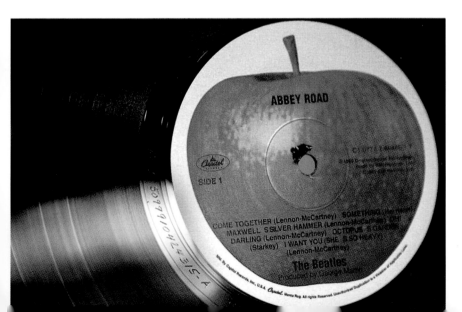

The next day, John asked Leary if there was anything that he could do to help him in his campaign and was asked if he could write a song to be used in commercials and performed at rallies. Leary's slogan was 'come together, join the party' – the 'come together' part coming from the *I Ching*, the Chinese book of changes. "There was obviously a double meaning there," said Leary. "It was come together and join the party – not a political party but a celebration of life."

John immediately picked up his guitar and began building on the phrase: 'Come together right now, Don't come tomorrow, Don't come alone, Come together right now over me, All that I can tell you, Is you gotta be free.' After coming up with a few more versions along the same lines, he made a demo tape and handed it to Leary.

Leary had the song played on alternative radio stations throughout California and began to think of it as his own. However, unknown to him, John had returned to England and within seven weeks had recorded a version with the Beatles. In October, it was released on the flip side of 'Something', the first single to be taken from Abbey Road.

Leary's campaign to become governor of California came to an abrupt halt in December 1969, when he was charged with possessing marijuana and eventually imprisoned. It was while in prison that Leary first heard *Abbey Road* on a local rock station and 'Come Together' came as a complete surprise. "Although the new version was certainly a musical and lyrical improvement on my campaign song, I was a bit miffed that Lennon had passed me over this way... When I sent a mild protest to John, he replied with typical Lennon charm and wit that he was a tailor and I was a customer who had ordered a suit and never returned. So he sold it to someone else."

The recorded version was largely made up in the studio, the swampy New Orleans bass having been added by Paul. Two of the song lines referring to 'old flat top' were lifted from Chuck Berry's 'You Can't Catch Me' and John was later sued for plagiarism. It was hard to deny where the words had come from, although, in this new context, they were nothing more than an affectionate nod towards the music of his youth. John strenuously denied any musical theft.

The conflict was resolved when John promised to record three songs belonging to the publisher of 'You Can't Catch Me'. He fulfilled this promise when he recorded Berry's 'Sweet Little Sixteen' and 'You Can't Catch Me' for his *Rock'n'Roll* album and Lee Dorsey's 'Ya Ya' on *Walls and Bridges*.

COME TOGETHER
Written:
Lennon/
McCartney
Length: 4' 20"
UK release:
Abbey Road
album, September
26, 1969
US release:
Abbey Road
album, October 1,
1969

SOMETHING

'Something' was the first Beatles' A side to be written by George. Its sources of inspiration were Ray Charles, who he imagined singing it, and a 1968 album track by James Taylor titled 'Something In The Way She Moves', and his wife Pattie.

James Taylor, an American, was signed to the Apple label and his eponymous first album was produced by Peter Asher between July and October 1968. Paul played bass on one track. 'Something In The Way She Moves' was the last track on the first side of the album and the opening lines were: 'There's something in the way she moves, Or looks my way or calls my name, That seems to leave this troubled world behind.'

The White Album was being recorded at Abbey Road at exactly the same time as Taylor was recording at Trident Studios in London's

'Come Together' began life as a campaign song for LSD guru Timothy Leary when he ran for governor of California against Ronald Reagan.

Soho. Indeed, on October 3, George was at Trident recording 'Savoy Truffle' with Paul and Ringo and probably heard the track then.

"I've always assumed George must have heard it but I never actually spoke to him about it," says Taylor. "I'd written 'Something In The Way She Moves' about two years before I recorded it and, strangely enough I'd wanted to call it 'I Feel Fine', but of course that was a Beatles' track.

"I often notice traces of other people's work in my own songs," Taylor continues. "If George either consciously or unconsciously took a line from one of my songs then I find it very flattering. It's certainly not an unusual thing to happen. I'd made a tape of 'Something In The Way She Moves' and about seven other songs about a couple of months before I met Peter Asher. I know Paul listened to it at Apple but I'm not sure who else listened to it."

The basic writing of 'Something' must have taken place in October because George has said that he worked it out on piano in Studio 1, while Paul was overdubbing in Studio 2. The only reason it wasn't included on the White Album was because the track selection had already been completed.

George first offered 'Something' to Joe Cocker and Jackie Lomax but then, in May 1969, decided to record it with the Beatles for *Abbey Road*. 'Something' was an enormously successful song for George, becoming the second most covered Beatles' song after 'Yesterday' (Ray Charles and Smokey Robinson both did versions) and giving him his first American Top 10 hit.

It had always been assumed that he wrote the song about Pattie but in a 1996 interview he said, "I didn't. I just wrote it and then somebody put together a video that used some footage of me and Pattie, Paul and Linda, Ringo and Maureen and John and Yoko… actually, when I wrote it I was thinking of Ray Charles." However, Pattie still believes that he had her in mind. "He always told me that it was about me," she says.

SOMETHING

Written:	Harrison
Length:	3' 03"
UK release:	*Abbey Road* album, September 26, 1969
US release:	*Abbey Road* album, October 1, 1969

MAXWELL'S SILVER HAMMER

**MAXWELL'S
SILVER HAMMER**
Written:
Lennon/
McCartney
Length: 3' 27"
UK release:
Abbey Road
album, September
26, 1969
US RELEASE:
Abbey Road
album, October 1,
1969

A song, driven by strong rhymes, in which medical student Maxwell Edison uses his silver hammer to kill first his girlfriend, then a lecturer and finally a judge. Delivered in a jaunty, vaudevillian style, the only indication of Paul's recent avant-garde leanings was the mention of 'pataphysics', a word invented by Alfred Jarry, the French pioneer of absurd theatre, to describe a branch of metaphysics.

"John told me that 'Maxwell's Silver Hammer' was about the law of karma," says former Apple employee Tony King. "We were talking one day about 'Instant Karma' (John's 1970 single with Yoko Ono and the Plastic Ono Band) because something had happened where he'd been clobbered and he'd said that this was an example of instant karma. I asked him whether he believed that theory. He said that he did and that 'Maxwell's Silver Hammer' was the first song that they'd made about that. He said that the idea behind the song was that the minute you do something that's not right, Maxwell's silver hammer will come down on your head."

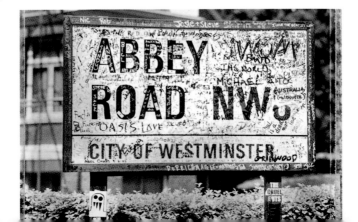

Beatles fans have for years covered the Abbey Road street sign in graffiti.

OH! DARLING

Paul wanted his voice to sound raw on 'Oh! Darling', so he sang it through again and again each day for a week before finally recording it. "I wanted it to sound as though I'd been performing it on stage all week," he said.

Inspired by the rock'n'roll ballads of the late Fifties, Jackie Wilson's in particular, it was a simple song pleading for a loved one to stay in exchange for lifelong devotion.

John never rated Paul's job on vocals and reckoned he could have done better. "It was more my style than his," he said.

OCTOPUS'S GARDEN

Ringo's second (and last) Beatles' song was inspired by a family holiday in Sardinia which he took in 1968 on board Peter Sellers' yacht. After Ringo had turned down the offer of an octopus lunch, the vessel's captain started to tell him all he knew about the life of octopuses.

"He told me how they go around the sea bed picking up stones and shiny objects to build gardens with," said Ringo. "I thought this was fabulous because at the time I just wanted to be under the sea too. I wanted to get out of it for a while."

To most listeners, it was a children's seaside song in the vein of 'Yellow Submarine' but, in 1969, George revealed that there were hidden dimensions. Even though Ringo only knew three chords on the piano, George said, the drummer was writing "cosmic songs without really noticing it."

OH! DARLING
Written: Lennon/McCartney
Length: 3' 26"
UK release: *Abbey Road* album, September 26, 1969
US release: *Abbey Road* album, October 1, 1969

OCTOPUS'S GARDEN
Written: Starr
Length: 2' 51"
UK release: *Abbey Road* album, September 26, 1969
US release: *Abbey Road* album, October 1, 1969

I WANT YOU

I WANT YOU
Written:
Lennon/
McCartney
Length: 7' 47"
UK release:
Abbey Road album,
September 26,
1969
US release:
Abbey Road album,
October 1, 1969

Consisting only of the repeated title line and the information that the desire is driving John mad, the lyric of 'I Want You' was once read out on BBC TV's current affairs programme *24 Hours* as an example of the banalities of pop music.

This incensed John, who was convinced that its simplicity made it superior to 'Eleanor Rigby' and 'I Am The Walrus'. To him, this was not a reversion to mindless monosyllabic pop but simply economy of language.

'I Want You' was written as a love song to Yoko. John admitted the influence she had on his new style of writing, saying that eventually he wanted to compose a perfect song using only one word. A 1964 poem of Yoko's consisted of the single word 'Water'.

133

Ringo wrote 'Octopus's Garden' (left) after an informative encounter with the captain of Peter Seller's yacht.

HERE COMES THE SUN

Written by George, 'Here Comes The Sun' was an expression of delight at being able to slip away from the interminable business meetings which were now taking up so much of the Beatles' time.

In January 1969, John and Yoko met with music business manager Allen Klein and shortly afterwards declared that he would be looking after their business affairs, despite the fact that the New York lawyer John Eastman, brother of Linda, had recently been brought in to represent the Beatles collectively. This was the beginning of a bitter drawn-out conflict over who should manage the Beatles and what should be done about the chaotic state of their finances. Despite the tremendous sales of Beatles' music over the past six years, John claimed, "all of us could be broke in six months".

Klein offered to restructure Apple, organize a takeover bid for the shares the Beatles didn't own in Northern Songs and renegotiate a better royalty deal with EMI. He was able to persuade John, George and Ringo of his ability to do these things but Paul remained loyal to Eastman. As a result the Beatles' existence was now under threat and the frequent meetings at Apple were fraught with tension. One morning in the early spring, George decided it was all getting a bit too much like school, and so he took a day off from the round table routine and went to see his friend Eric Clapton at his country home in Ewhurst, Surrey.

Borrowing one of Eric's acoustic guitars, George took a walk around the gardens and, basking in the first real sunshine of the year, he felt a sudden flush of optimism and started to write 'Here Comes The Sun'. "It was such a great release for me simply being out in the sun," said George at the time. "The song just came to me."

The arrival of Allan Klein in the Beatles' world led to a period of damaging in-fighting.

HERE COMES THE SUN
Written:
Harrison
Length: 3' 05"
UK release:
Abbey Road
album, September 26, 1969
US release:
Abbey Road
album, October 1, 1969

BECAUSE

John was relaxing on a sofa at home, while Yoko played the first movement of Beethoven's Piano Sonata No 14 in C Sharp Minor ('Moonlight Sonata') on the grand piano. John has said that he asked her if she could play the same chords in reverse order. This she did, and it proved to be the inspiration for 'Because'.

The similarity between the opening of the 'Moonlight Sonata' and 'Because' is striking, although close scrutiny reveals it to be a straightforward lift rather than the reversal of notes John suggested. Musicologist Wilfrid Mellers, author of *Twilight Of The Gods: The Music of the Beatles* puts it this way, "The affinity between the enveloping, arpeggiated C sharp minor triads, with the sudden shift to the flat supertonic, is, in the Lennon and Beethoven examples, unmistakable."

There was a touch of irony in the idea of a Beatle borrowing from Beethoven because there was a common perception at the time that rock'n'roll was antithetical to classical music and that no one could genuinely appreciate both. It also probably didn't help that the Beatles had recorded Chuck Berry's 'Roll Over Beethoven', an irreverent piece of advice to classical composers asking them to make way for rock'n'roll.

One of the first questions the Beatles were always asked in America was, 'What do you think of Beethoven?' It was Ringo who answered. "I love him," he said. "Especially his poems." But it was John, in particular, who came to regard Beethoven as the supreme composer, and one with whom he felt kinship. By 1969, he was no longer trying to be the artistic equal of Elvis or the Rolling Stones, but of Picasso, Van Gogh, Dylan Thomas and Beethoven.

BECAUSE
Written:
Lennon/
McCartney
Length: 2' 45"
UK release:
Abbey Road
album, September
26, 1969
US release:
Abbey Road
album, October 1,
1969

YOU NEVER GIVE
ME YOUR MONEY

'You Never Give Me Your Money' announced the medley of half-finished songs which dominate the second side of *Abbey Road*. Paul collected the songs and carefully worked out a way of linking them together. 'You Never Give Me Your Money' itself is made up of three distinct fragments. The first, which develops the line in the title, was an allusion to the Beatles' financial problems saying that instead of money all they ever seemed to get was 'funny paper'.

"That's what we get," said George. "We get bits of paper saying how much is earned and what this and that is but we never actually get it in pounds, shillings and pence. We've all got a big house and a car and an office but to actually get the money we've earned seems impossible."

The next fragment, which mentions being penniless after leaving college, may have referred to the same problems but was written in the jolly, nostalgic style of Paul's 'woke up/ got out of bed' section of 'A Day In The Life'. The final piece was about the freedom of Paul's new life with Linda, where he could just pack the car and drive out of town leaving his worries behind.

YOU NEVER GIVE ME YOUR MONEY

Written:	Lennon/McCartney
Length:	4' 02"
UK release:	*Abbey Road* album, September 26, 1969
US release:	*Abbey Road* album, October 1, 1969

SUN KING

Fleetwood Mac's hit 'Albatross' exerted a major sonic influence over 'Sun King'.

As with 'Being For The Benefit Of Mr Kite!', John's opinions on 'Sun King' came to alter over the years but this time, changing from good to bad. In 1971, he referred to it as something that had come to him in a dream, implying that it was an inspired piece of work. By 1980, it had been revalued as just another piece of 'garbage'.

Historically, the Sun King was Louis XIV of France and it could have been he who John dreamt about, a dream wherein the King entered his palace to find all his guests were laughing and happy. Nancy Mitford had recently published a biography of Louis which was titled *The Sun King* and John may have read it or at least seen it. It may also have been a jokey reference to George's song 'Here Comes The Sun'.

The closing lines of the song are composed of those Italian, Spanish and Portuguese words which tourists pick up, strung together in no particular order – 'paparazzi', 'obrigado', 'parasol', 'mi amore'. The original title of the song was 'Los Paranoias'.

According to George, the point of musical departure was Fleetwood Mac's 'Albatross', a dreamy instrumental which had been a British Top 10 hit in the early part of 1969.

SUN KING
Written:
Lennon/
McCartney
Length: 2' 26"
UK release:
Abbey Road
album, September 26, 1969
US release:
Abbey Road
album, October 1, 1969

MEAN MR MUSTARD

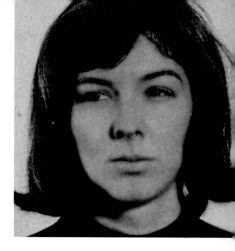

John said that 'Mean Mr Mustard' was inspired by a newspaper story about a miser who concealed his cash wherever he could in order to prevent people forcing him to spend it. The line about stuffing a 'ten bob note' (a British ten shilling note) up his nose John admitted was his own invention, claiming that it had absolutely nothing to do with snorting cocaine.

Tony Bramwell believes another colourful London character also provided John with inspiration for this song. "There was an old 'bag lady' who used to hang around the Knightsbridge end of Hyde Park, close to the army barracks," he remembers. "She had all her possessions in plastic bags and slept in the park. I'm sure that she had something to do with the song."

The reference to a 'dirty old man' in the last line may have been to the character of Albert Steptoe in the BBC TV situation comedy *Steptoe & Son* (1962–1974) who was always referred to by his son Harold as a 'You dirty old man'. It became a catch phrase in Britain around the same time that the actor who played Steptoe, Wilfrid Brambell, took on the part of Paul's grandfather in *A Hard Day's Night*. (This explains the many references in the movie to Paul's granddad being 'very clean'.)

Written in India, 'Mean Mr Mustard' was recorded with 'Sun King' in one continuous piece. In the original version, Mr Mustard had a sister called Shirley but John changed it to Pam when he realized that it could more easily segue into 'Polythene Pam'.

Royston Ellis's lover, Stephanie, was one of two major inspirations behind John's song 'Polythene Pam' (right).

MEAN MR MUSTARD
Written: Lennon/McCartney
Length: 1' 06"
UK release: *Abbey Road* album, September 26, 1969
US release: *Abbey Road* album, October 1, 1969

POLYTHENE PAM

Although John initially insisted that 'Polythene Pam' was about "a mythical Liverpool scrubber (promiscuous girl or groupie) dressed up in her jackboots and kilt", the song was actually based on two people who he had known. The name came from Pat Dawson (then Pat Hodgett), a Beatles' fan from the Cavern Club days who, because of her habit of eating polythene, was known to the group as Polythene Pat. "I started going to see the Beatles in 1961 when I was 14 and I got quite friendly with them," she remembers. "If they were playing out of town they'd give me a lift back home in their van. It was about the same time that I started getting called Polythene Pat. It's embarrassing really. I just used to eat polythene all the time. I'd tie it in knots and then eat it. Sometimes I even used to burn it and then eat it when it got cold. Then I had a friend who got a job in a polythene bag factory, which was wonderful because it meant I had a constant supply."

But Polythene Pat never dressed up in polythene bags as the song says. That little quirk was taken from an incident involving a girl called Stephanie, who John met in the Channel Islands while on tour in August 1963.

Although John wouldn't elaborate when he spoke to *Playboy* in 1980, he did supply a few clues. "(Polythene Pam) was me remembering a little event with a woman in Jersey, and a man who was England's answer to Allen Ginsberg, who gave us our first exposure…"

England's answer to American beat poet Ginsberg turned out to be Royston Ellis, a young writer who first met the Beatles in May or June of 1960 when invited to read poetry at Liverpool University. What John went on reluctantly to tell *Playboy* was that Ellis was the first person to introduce the Beatles to drugs when he showed them how to get high from the strips inside a Benzedrine inhaler.

The "little event with a woman", as John described it, actually took place on the Channel island of Guernsey, not Jersey, when John met up with Ellis who had a summer job there as a ferry boat engineer. After the Beatles' concerts at the Auditorium in Guernsey on August 8, Ellis and his girlfriend Stephanie took John back to the attic flat Ellis was renting and this is where the polythene came into the story. "(Ellis) said Miss X (a girl he wanted me to meet) dressed up in polythene," John later remembered. "She did. She didn't wear jackboots and kilts. I just sort of elaborated. Perverted sex in a polythene bag. I was just looking for something to write about."

Ellis, who now lives in Sri Lanka and writes travel books, can't recall any 'perverted sex' but he can recall the night spent in a bed with Stephanie and John. "We'd read all these things about leather and we didn't have any leather but I had my oilskins and we had some polythene bags from somewhere," he says. "We all dressed up in them and wore them in bed. John stayed the night with us in the same bed. I don't think anything very exciting happened and we all wondered what the fun was in being 'kinky'. It was probably more my idea than John's. It could have all happened because in a poetry booklet of mine which I had dedicated to the Beatles there was a poem with the lines: 'I long to have sex between black leather sheets, And ride shivering motorcycles between your thighs.'

"At the time, it meant nothing to me. It was just one event during a very eventful time of my life," Ellis adds. Besides being a poet, Ellis was a pundit on teenage life and a chronicler of emergent British rock'n'roll. When they met, he had just completed *The Big Beat Scene*, an excellent survey of late Fifties British beat music.

POLYTHENE PAM

Written:	Lennon/McCartney
Length:	1' 12"
UK release:	*Abbey Road* album, September 26, 1969
US release:	*Abbey Road* album, October 1, 1969

John was fascinated by Ellis because he stood at the converging point of rock'n'roll and literature. Ellis arranged for the Beatles to back him early on at a beat music and poetry event at the Jacaranda Club. In July 1960, *Record Mirror* reported that 'the bearded sage' was thinking of bringing a Liverpool group called the 'Beetles' to London to play behind him as he performed his poetry. "I was quite a star for them at that time because I had come up from London and that was a world they didn't really know about," says Ellis. "I stayed with them for about a week in their flat at Gambier Terrace. John was fascinated by the fact that I was a poet and that led to deep conversations."

Shortly after introducing John to the delights of polythene, Ellis left England and has spent much of the time since travelling. So far removed has he been from the British pop scene, that he had never even heard 'Polythene Pam' until contacted for this book. He does recall with some pride, though, that in 1973 John wrote to the alternative newspaper *International Times* to correct them about the circumstances of the Beatles' first drug experiences: "The first dope, from a Benzedrine inhaler, was given the Beatles (John, George, Paul and Stuart) by an English cover version of Allen Ginsberg – one Royston Ellis, known as 'beat poet'…So, give the saint his due."

141

Stephanie reads while 'beat poet' Royston Ellis takes a nap in the Channel Islands in 1963, the year Ellis met up again with John.

SHE CAME IN THROUGH THE BATHROOM WINDOW

This song was inspired by the activities of an Apple Scruff who climbed into Paul's house in St John's Wood when he was away for the day. "We were bored, he was out and so we decided to pay him a visit," remembers Diane Ashley. "We found a ladder in his garden and stuck it up at the bathroom window which he'd left slightly open. I was the one who climbed up and got in."

Once she was inside the house, she opened the front door and let the rest of the girls in. Fellow Apple Scruff Margo Bird remembers: "They rummaged around and took some clothes. People didn't usually take anything of real value but I think this time a lot of photographs and negatives were taken. There were really two groups of Apple Scruffs – those who would break in and those who would just wait outside with cameras and autograph books. I used to take Paul's dog for a walk and got to know him quite well. I was eventually offered a job at Apple. I started by making the tea and ended up in the promotions department working with Tony King."

Paul asked Margo if she could retrieve any of his belongings. "I knew who had done it and I discovered that a lot of the stuff had already gone to America," she said. "But I knew that there was one picture he particularly wanted back – a colour-tinted picture of him in a Thirties frame. I knew who had taken this and got it back for him."

Paul completed 'She Came In Through The Bathroom Window' in June 1968 during a trip to America to do business with Capitol Records. It was here that he resumed his relationship with Linda Eastman, whom he'd been introduced to the previous summer in London and had since met in New York.

SHE CAME IN THROUGH THE BATHROOM WINDOW
Written: Lennon/McCartney
Length: 1'57"
UK release: *Abbey Road* album, September 26, 1969
US release: *Abbey Road* album, October 1, 1969

Paul wrote 'She Came In Through The Bathroom Window' about some of the band's obsessive fans.

"Paul and Heather and I were in New York going to the airport to come back to England," remembers Linda. "The name of the taxi driver talking to us was Eugene Quits, so then Paul wrote the line 'So I quite the police department.'"

According to Carol Bedford, an Apple Scruff who wrote the book *Waiting For The Beatles*, Paul later said to her: "I've written a song about the girls who broke in. It's called 'She Came In Through The Bathroom Window'." Diane was surprised to have become the subject of a Beatles' song. "I didn't believe it at first because he'd hated it so much when we broke in," she says. "But then I suppose anything can inspire a song, can't it? I know that all his neighbours rang him when they saw we'd got in and I'm sure that gave rise to the lines, 'Sunday's on the 'phone to Monday/Tuesday's on the 'phone to me'."

Now married with four teenage children, Diane keeps a framed photo of herself with Paul on her kitchen shelf and looks back on her days as an Apple Scruff with affection. "I don't regret any of it. I had a great time, a really great time."

GOLDEN SLUMBERS

Paul was at his father's house in Cheshire tinkering around on the piano. Flicking through a songbook belonging to his step-sister Ruth (James McCartney had since remarried), he came across the traditional lullaby 'Golden Slumbers'. Unable to read the music, he went ahead and made up his own melody, adding new words as he went along.

'Golden Slumbers' was written by the English writer and dramatist Thomas Dekker, who was a contemporary of Shakespeare. The song was first published in *The Pleasant Comedy of Old Fortunatus* (1600).

A Londoner born around 1570, Dekker was the author of *The Shoemaker's Holiday* (1600), *The Honest Whore* (1604), *The Gull's Hornbook* (1609), *The Roaring Girl* (1611) and the posthumously published *The Syn's Darling* (1656).

For 'Golden Slumbers' Paul wrote a new melody for an old British lullaby.

GOLDEN SLUMBERS

Written:	Lennon/McCartney
Length:	1'31"
UK release:	*Abbey Road* album, September 26, 1969
US release:	*Abbey Road* album, October 1, 1969

HER MAJESTY

Written by Paul in Scotland, 'Her Majesty' was originally part of the medley, coming between 'Mean Mr Mustard' and 'Polythene Pam' but, on hearing a playback, Paul didn't like it and asked for it to be edited out.

The engineer who cut it out then recycled it to the end of the tape so that it wouldn't be destroyed. Paul must have heard another playback with 'Her Majesty' now tacked on as an apparent afterthought. He liked it enough to keep it there. Because the edit was only meant to be rough, the last chord of 'Mean Mr Mustard' was pressed into service to start 'Her Majesty', which ends abruptly because its own final note was left behind at the beginning of 'Polythene Pam'.

The Beatles met Queen Elizabeth to receive their MBEs on October 26, 1965. Afterwards, asked what they thought of her, Paul answered: "She's lovely. She was very friendly. She was just like a mum to us." Years later, Paul confessed to having had a crush on the young Elizabeth when he was a boy.

'Her Majesty' has the dubious distinction of being the final track on the last album the Fab Four were ever to record together.

HER MAJESTY

Written:	Lennon/McCartney
Length:	0' 23"
UK release:	*Abbey Road* album, September 26, 1969
US release:	*Abbey Road* album, October 1, 1969

CARRY THAT WEIGHT

Although 'Carry That Weight' appears to be just another song in the medley and is credited as such on the album, it was in fact recorded with 'Golden Slumbers' as a single. It's a nice touch because it brings the sequence back to where it started with the subject of money, business and the burdens of being a superstar.

The lyric expressed Paul's fears about the Beatles in their twilight days. He later said that the arguments over finance and management plunged him into the "darkest hours" of his life so far. The atmosphere around the Beatles had changed from light to heavy. "At certain times things get to me so much that I can't be upbeat any more and that was one of the times," he told his biographer Barry Miles.

CARRY THAT WEIGHT
Written:
Lennon/
McCartney
Length: 1' 36"
UK release:
Abbey Road
album, September
26, 1969
US release:
Abbey Road
album, October 1,
1969

In the later years, the Beatles' intra-band tensions affected even Paul's famously upbeat demanour, as related in 'Carry That Weight'.

THE END

As the final proper track on the last album recorded by the Beatles, 'The End' was to become the song which signed off their studio career. Philosophical to the last, Paul says that ultimately the love you 'take' is equal to the love you 'make'. He may have been saying no more that 'you take out what you put in', but John was sufficiently impressed to declare it a "very cosmic line" proving that "if Paul wants to, he can think."

Paul saw the couplet as a musical equivalent of the rhyming couplets with which Shakespeare ended some of his plays, a summary and also a signal that the events of the drama were now ended.

It certainly provided a neat symmetry to their recording career – which started with the gawky pleadings of lovesick teenagers in 'Love Me Do', and matured to reveal enigmatic words of wisdom from the group who transformed popular music.

THE END

Written:	Lennon/McCartney
Length:	2' 19"
UK release:	*Abbey Road* album, September 26, 1969
US release:	*Abbey Road* album, October 1, 1969

LIVE AT THE BBC

In 1982 Kevin Howlett looked through the BBC's archives of radio sessions with the Beatles and produced a programme called *Beatles At The Beeb*. Shortly afterwards, discussions began between EMI and the BBC to get the material released. However, it wasn't until 1994 that the right climate prevailed between the Beatles, Apple and EMI which enabled the project to be actualised.

Howlett took the BBC tapes to George Martin at Abbey Road where Martin digitally remastered the 58 tracks which survived from the 88 songs which the Beatles had played live on BBC radio. In fact, only 57 of the tracks had survived in the BBC archives. The 58th was secured from a fan who had contacted Howlett in 1988, during the transmission of another Beatles series.

These robust live performances didn't have the benefit of multitrack recording facilities, overdubs or remixes and so provide an undoctored example of what the Beatles sounded like during the peak of their performing career. John and Paul learned to write songs by emulating the great singles of their youth. Trying these cover versions out on audiences taught them what worked and helped them to understand why. Bit by bit they began to drop the cover versions for songs of their own which created the same mood.

Live At The BBC illustrates this growth. Of the songs they cover, 76% were from between 1954 and 1959, when they were serving their apprenticeship in Liverpool. Almost half the cover songs were written by a handful of writers they revered – Chuck Berry, Little Richard, Carl Perkins, Goffin and King and Leiber and Stoller.

The double album *Live At The BBC* was released in November 1994 and went on to sell over 8 million copies.

I'LL BE ON MY WAY

A very early Beatles song, 'I'll Be On My Way' was composed in youthful emulation of Buddy Holly.

'I'll Be On My Way' was the only unreleased Lennon-McCartney song to be included on Live At The BBC and, as such, the first Lennon-McCartney song played by the Beatles to be released since May 1970.

Written by Paul in 1961 in emulation of Buddy Holly it was included in the group's repertoire over the next two years but wasn't played at the Decca audition, an indication that it had already fallen out of favour. It was given to their stable mate Billy J. Kramer who used it as the flip side of 'Do You Want To Know A Secret?' in April 1963.

The lyric serves as a reminder that the Beatles didn't start out as artistic visionaries but simply rearranged existing clichés. Here 'June light' turns to 'moon light' (naturally) and the lovelorn narrator is forced into exile where 'golden rivers flow' and 'the winds don't blow'. It sounds like the rim of an active volcano, but maybe Paul had something else in mind.

John, typically, poured scorn on the song when asked about it in 1980: it was precisely the sort of pop that had always made him uncomfortable because it stifled the individual point of view with a raft of stock phrases. Paul wasn't quite so harsh when he looked back. It was "a bit too June-moon" he conceded, but it had "worked out quite well" for the group in their early shows.

I'LL BE ON MY WAY

Written:
Lennon/
McCartney
Length: 1' 57"
UK release:
*Live at the BBC
album*, November
30, 1994
US release:
*Live at the BBC
album*, November
30, 1994

ANTHOLOGY 1-3

The three double albums that comprise the *Anthology* set owe their genesis to an exercise in 1984 when engineer John Barrett was given the task of collating all the Beatles material in EMI's archives. Out of hundreds of hours of recordings he identified three unreleased tracks. EMI made test pressings and approached the remaining Beatles with the suggestion of an album. At the time, no agreement on a release could be reached.

Five years later, in an unrelated move, Apple's long-time manager Neil Aspinall revived a documentary idea he'd abandoned in 1969. He wanted to collect together all the best film footage of the Beatles for a television series that would tell their story in their words. He wanted the remaining Beatles to come together and record some new incidental music. The project would be called *The Long And Winding Road.*

The album of unreleased songs and the documentary series eventually coalesced into *Anthology.* The planned incidental music was dropped in favour of recording two new Beatles tracks. "As the thought of the three of us sitting down in a studio got nearer, I got cold feet about it," said Paul. "I thought, Does the world need a three-quarter Beatle record? But what if John was on, the three of us and John, like a real new record? If only we could pull off the impossible, that would be more fun, a bigger challenge."

The apparently impossible was pulled off when Yoko agreed to let them use two demo cassettes of unfinished songs by John as the basis for new Beatles tracks. These eventually became singles which helped to promote not only the six-hour documentary series but the *Anthology* albums.

Ringo, Paul, George
and producer George
Martin reconvene in
1994 for *Anthology*.

Anthology was not a soundtrack to the documentary series but an aural counterpart made up of alternative takes, unreleased tracks, live performances, early demos and brief snatches of interview. Out of the 139 songs on the collection, 28 were cover versions.

The greatest interest was naturally in the 21 new Beatles compositions, some of which had only previously been heard performed by other artists or on rare bootlegs. These ranged from poor-quality home recordings that were purely of historical value to completed studio tracks that had been ousted from albums only for reasons of space.

The general critical response to these rarities was that the Beatles original judgment to drop them or give them away had been sound. They could probably have had a hit with 'Come And Get It' and it's hard to see why 'Not Guilty' didn't find a place on *The White Album* but otherwise none of these 'new' songs enhanced their reputation. They merely confirmed what we had assumed, which was that the Beatles had already given us their best.

FREE AS A BIRD

'Free As A Bird' was essentially a novelty single designed to attract attention to the *Anthology* project. The novelty was that it would be the first new Beatles single in 25 years and would, in sound at least, reunite the most popular pop group the world has known.

There was feverish media excitement surrounding the release of the record, which was encouraged by EMI's publicity department. An early press release read, "The single, copies of which are currently under armed guard outside the UK, will be released worldwide on MONDAY DECEMBER 4 [1995]."

Nothing could hope to live up to these expectations but, in the event, 'Free As A Bird' was plausibly Beatles-sounding (circa 1969) although obviously hampered by the restraints of having been built around a discarded fragment of a John Lennon song that had been recorded on a cassette machine.

The events that led to the recording began on January 1, 1994 when Paul called Yoko to wish her a Happy New Year. This act of reconciliation led to further conversations and then a meeting when Paul attended John's induction into the Rock'n'Roll Hall Of Fame. During this time together they discussed the possibility of the remaining Beatles working on John's home demos. Yoko offered three tracks for consideration – 'Real Love', 'Grow Old With Me' and 'Free As A Bird'.

"I liked 'Free As A Bird' immediately," Paul said. "I liked the melody. It had strong chords and it really appealed to me…The great thing was that John hadn't finished it. On the middle eight he was just blocking out lyrics that he didn't have yet. That meant that we had to come up with something, and that now I was actually working 'with John'."

'Free As A Bird' was an expression of John's love of his happy home life with Yoko and Sean.

John probably first worked on the song at home in New York during the latter part of 1977. On October 4th of that year he and Yoko held a press conference in Japan to announce that they were both putting their careers on hold to concentrate on raising their son Sean.

Several of the songs he began during this period dealt with his new life as a house husband. In 'I'm Stepping Out', 'Watching The Wheels', 'Beautiful Boy' and 'Cleanup Time' he wrote of the strange sense of freedom he felt in abandoning the life of a celebrity for domestic duties.

Like many people psychologically wounded in early life, John craved attention and then spurned it when it came. Interviewed by *Rolling Stone* in 1970 his first comment was, "If I had the capabilities of being something other than I am, I would. It's no fun being an artist." His final comment, after being asked how he saw himself at 64, was in a similar vein. "I hope we're a nice old couple living off the coast of Ireland or something like that – looking at our scrapbook of madness."

For John, a stable family home had been the one thing that had always eluded him. With Sean and Yoko, he was determined to hang on to what he had got. 'Free As A Bird' was written to express his delight at being set free from the demands of celebrity and from the artistic pressure of having to compete with his earlier selves. He was, as he sings, 'home and dry'.

For the middle section of the song John had only the couplet 'Whatever happened to/The life that we once knew?', lines reminiscent of the belief he had expressed in 'Help!', 'Strawberry

The surviving Beatles pretended that John was still alive as they recorded *Anthology*.

Fields Forever' and 'In My Life' that his childhood was the most idyllic time of his life. Paul's additional lines subvert this train of thought, turning it into a longing for healed relationships – presumably his own with John.

Recording took place in February and March of 1994 at Paul's studio in Sussex with production credits being shared between the Beatles and former Electric Light Orchestra vocalist/guitarist Jeff Lynne. John's original cassette was transferred to tape and the sound digitally remastered. "We then took the liberty of beefing the song up with different chord changes and different arrangements," said George Harrison.

The project was approached as if John was still alive and that he and Paul were still working on each other's unfinished songs. "We came up with this holiday scenario," said Paul. "I rang up Ringo and said let's pretend that John's gone on holiday and he's sent us a cassette and said, 'Finish it up for me'."

George Martin, who had produced every other Beatles single, gave it a cautious blessing but felt that it lacked dynamics because they hadn't been able to successfully separate the piano and vocals on the original cassette and had put it in a rigid time beat to make overdubbing easier.

"They stretched it and compressed it and put it around until it got to a regular waltz control click and then they were done," he said. "The result was that, in order to conceal the bad bits, they had to plaster it fairly heavily so that what you ended up with was quite a thick homogeneous sound that hardly stops."

'Free As A Bird' reached number two in the British charts and number six in America.

FREE AS A BIRD
Written: Lennon
Length: 4' 24"
UK single release: December 4, 1995
UK chart position: 2
US single release: December 4, 1995
US chart position: 6

REAL LOVE

'Real Love' was a song John had worked on for at least two years and, although many people weren't aware of it, a version was used in the 1988 soundtrack to Andrew Solt's documentary *Imagine*.

It began as a song called 'Real Life', the verses of which later became 'I'm Stepping Out', posthumously released on *Milk And Honey*. The remaining chorus – 'It's real life/Yes, it's real life' – he obviously thought too good to throw away. The theme of the tune – I'm back to what really counts in life – was the essential theme of all his post-Beatle work. He was still stripping away myths, dispensing with the unnecessary and in this case, getting down to the reality of kitchens, cigarettes, babies, newspapers and early morning blues.

The revamped song was coming closer to the version that the Beatles would work on. The references to 'little girls and boys' and 'little plans and schemes' were now there.

When he finally changed the chorus from 'real life' to 'real love' the theme became the transforming love of Yoko Ono. He said many times in interview that he felt that she was the woman that all his longings for love and acceptance had been directed towards even before he met her. She was the 'girl with kaleidoscope eyes'. She was, as he wrote in his essay *The Ballad Of John And Yoko*, "Someone who I had already known, but somehow had lost."

In February 1995, Jeff Lynne deleted extraneous noises on John's cassette copy of 'Real Love' and transferred the mono recording to two 24-track analogue tapes at Paul's Sussex studio. Paul, George and Ringo added guitars, drums, bass, percussion and backing vocals. At one point Paul even used his upright bass which once belonged to Bill Black and was used on Elvis Presley's 'Heartbreak Hotel'.

REAL LOVE
Written: Lennon
Length: 3' 54"
UK single release: March 4, 1996
UK chart position: 4
US single release: March 4, 1996
US chart position: 11

155

CHRISTMAS TIME (IS HERE AGAIN)

Particularly for the British, the Beatles became inextricably linked to the Christmases of the 1960s. Six of their albums were released to capitalise on the Christmas market and four of their singles were Christmas number ones. In 1963 and 1964 they presented special Christmas shows in London theatres which were a mixture of music and pantomime and had support acts ranging from the Yardbirds to Rolf Harris.

Between 1963 and 1969 they produced a flexidisc exclusively for members of their official fan club which offered spoken greetings from each Beatle and some light hearted conversation. The earliest messages were clearly scripted but as their music developed so did the discs. In 1965 they fooled around with a version of 'Auld Lang Syne' and the next year Paul wrote a mini-pantomime for the group.

'Christmas Time (Is Here Again)', the only original song written for fan club members, came out in 1967, the year that *Magical Mystery Tour* was being screened on Boxing Day. The unedited version, recorded on November 28th, was over six minutes long and parts of it were used to punctuate a satirical sketch written by all four Beatles.

Although it largely consists of a single line repeated like a musical mantra, 'Christmas Time (Is Here Again)' is illustrative of their fascination with children's songs and rhymes which began with 'Yellow Submarine' in 1966. This in part reflected nostalgia for the Liverpool of the 1940s but was also part of the psychedelic tendency to regress to simpler states of mind where it wasn't out of place for an adult to wear ripped jeans, blow bubbles and think buttercups were 'far out'.

In their early years, the band pandered to the Christmas market on an annual basis.

CHRISTMAS TIME (IS HERE AGAIN)
Written: Harrison/Lennon/McCartney/Starr
Length: 3' 03"
UK single release: December 4, 1995 on 'Free As A Bird' EP
US single release: December 4, 1995 on 'Free As A Bird' EP

IN SPITE OF ALL THE DANGER

A rough recording transferred from a slightly worn 78 rpm shellac disc cut in the spring or summer of 1958, this has historical value in that it is the earliest taping of the soon-to-be Beatles as well as being the group's first songwriting effort to make it into the archives.

It was recorded on a £400 portable tape recorder at a small studio housed in the terraced home of a 63-year-old electrical goods shop owner in the Kensington district of Liverpool. The Quarry Men, which then consisted of John, Paul, George, pianist John Duff Lowe and drummer Colin Hanton, paid 17 shillings and six pence (87p) to have two songs.cut.

The first song they chose was 'That'll Be The Day', a September 1957 hit in Britain for the Crickets (with Buddy Holly), and the second was the McCartney-Harrison number 'In Spite Of All The Danger'.

"It says on the label that it was me and George but I think it was written by me and George played the guitar solo," said Paul in 1995. "It was my song. It was very similar to an Elvis song."

It was in fact very similar to a particular Elvis song – 'Trying To Get To You' – which was written by Rose Marie McCoy and Margie Singleton and recorded by Elvis on July 11 1955. It was the only Sun recording by Elvis ever to use a piano and was released as a single in September 1956.

John Duff Lowe remembers 'In Spite Of All The Danger' as being the only original song the Quarry Men played at the time.

"I can well remember even at the rehearsal at his house in Forthlin Road Paul was quite specific about how he wanted it played and what he wanted the piano to do," he says. "There was no

IN SPITE OF ALL THE DANGER

Written:	Harrison/McCartney
Length:	2' 44"
UK release:	Anthology 1 album, November 21, 1995
US release:	Anthology 1 album, November 21, 1995

question of improvising. We were told what we had to play. There was a lot of arranging going on, even back then."

It was recorded on a single microphone and Lowe thinks that it must have gone straight to disc because he can't recall waiting around for it to be transferred from tape and there are mistakes in John's vocal which would otherwise have been corrected.

The disc was then passed on from member to member and eventually came down to Lowe who kept it in a sock drawer until 1981 when a colleague suggested to him that it might have some commercial value. He had it valued by Sotheby's which led to the discovery of the disc being reported by *Sunday Times* columnist Stephen Pile in July 1981.

"Before mid-day on that Sunday Paul McCartney had called my mum in Liverpool," says Lowe. "I eventually spoke to him on the 'phone and we had long conversations over the next few days because he wanted to buy it from me.

"I was living in Worcester at the time and he sent his solicitor and his business manager up. I deposited the disc in a small brief case at the local Barclay's Bank and we met up in a small room the bank kindly let me use. The deal was done, I handed the record over and we all went home."

Although Paul didn't have a specific project in mind at the time, part of the deal was that Lowe had to assign over all rights to the track and promise not to perform the song for the next fifteen years. "That took us up to August 1996," says Lowe. "Isn't it strange that two months later the final album in the *Anthology* set came out?"

YOU'LL BE MINE

Paul and John were at their most precocious on 'You'll Be Mine', the Goons-influenced first recording of a Lennon/McCartney song.

Recorded in the summer of 1960 on a borrowed tape machine at Paul's family home at Forthlin Road this is the first recording of a Lennon and McCartney song, although that's the extent of its interest. It sounds like nothing more than a couple of minutes of musical hilarity put together by teenagers in awe of the sound of their own voices.

Without a drummer but with the addition of fourth guitarist Stuart Sutcliffe, the group were rehearsing for their upcoming stint in Hamburg and decided on an Inkspots parody with John delivering a melodramatic spoken section that owed a lot to his fascination with the Goons. Appropriately, the whole tracks concludes with a wild squeal of laughter. You can almost imagine them wetting themselves as they played it back again and again.

YOU'LL BE MINE

Written:	Lennon/McCartney
Length:	1' 38"
UK release:	Anthology 1 album, November 21, 1995
US release:	Anthology 1 album, November 21, 1995

CAYENNE

Paul has said that the instrumental 'Cayenne', or 'Cayenne Pepper' as it was originally titled, was written before he met John, probably at the age of 14 when he got his first £15 guitar. Another instrumental he wrote around the same time, 'Cat's Walk', was recorded by the Chris Barber Band in 1967 as 'Cat Call'.

When Paul committed 'Cayenne' to tape in the summer of 1960 rock'n'roll instrumentals were a regular chart phenomenon. Since January there had been hit singles by Johnny and the Hurricanes, the Ventures, Duane Eddy, Bert Weedon, Sandy Nelson, Jerry Lordan, the John Barry Seven and the Shadows.

"It's not brilliant," Paul said recently of 'Cayenne', "But when you listen to it you can hear a lot of stuff I'm going to write. So, it's interesting from that point of view."

CAYENNE
Written:
McCartney
Length: 1' 13"
UK release:
Anthology 1 album,
November 21,
1995
US release:
Anthology 1
album, November
21, 1995

Paul wrote 'Cayenne" before even his 1957 first meeting with John.

CRY FOR A SHADOW

CRY FOR A
SHADOW
Written:
Harrison/Lennon
Length: 2' 22''
UK release:
Anthology 1 album,
November 21,
1995
US release:
Anthology 1
album, November
21, 1995

When this track was recorded in June 1961, Cliff Richard and The Shadows were Britain's premier rock and roll act. Since his first hit with 'Move It' in October 1958 Cliff had been in the Top Ten ten times and the Shadows were now making their own instrumental hits.

Although the Beatles found Cliff a bit too tame for their liking, they were early admirers of the Shadows. Paul learned the opening chords of 'Move It' from watching lead guitarist Hank Marvin's finger movements on the *Oh Boy!* TV show and, when Cliff first played the Liverpool Empire on October 12, 1958, Paul was in the audience.

'Cry For A Shadow', an instrumental intended to sound like mock Shadows, was credited to Harrison/Lennon. It was the Beatles' first composition to make it onto record when it appeared on Tony Sheridan's 1962 German album *My Bonnie* where the 'backing group' were listed as the Beat Brothers.

The composition came about by accident. Rory Storm was in Germany and had asked George to play him a recent Shadows hit – 'Apache' or 'Frightened City' – and George played something new, either because he couldn't remember the Shadows' tunes or as a joke on Storm. At first he called it 'Beatle Bop' but then, out of homage to his original inspiration, he called it 'Cry For A Shadow'.

"It doesn't sound like 'Frightened City' or 'Apache'," says Shadows guitarist Bruce Welch. "What it has in common with the Shadows is that it has the same instrumentation that we used but melodically it's nowhere near either of them.

"What I had heard was that it was done as a piss-take because at that time we had a stranglehold on the British group scene and we'd never been to Germany as almost every other group did." The song was recorded in Germany when the orchestra leader and record company producer Bert Kaempfert hired the Beatles for 300 Deutschmarks to back Sheridan on a Polydor record. Norwich-born Sheridan, a veteran of London's 2 I's coffee bar, had spent a lot of time in Germany and Kaempfert wanted him to do rocked-up versions of such standards as 'My Bonnie' and 'When The Saints Go Marching In'. The Beatles were allowed their own spot on 'Ain't She Sweet' and 'Cry For A Shadow'.

Brian Epstein, who was responsible for getting the Beatles out of leather jackets and into tailored suits, encouraged them to emulate the Shadows in their attire and on-stage courtesies. The two groups first met in 1963 at a party in London and in June of that year Hank, Bruce and Brian Locking came to Paul's 21st in Liverpool.

The band wrote 'Cry For A Shadow' in an attempt to replicate the sound of Cliff Richard's backing group, the Shadows.

LIKE DREAMERS DO

Merseybeat consisted largely of covers of recent American hits and selections from Buddy Holly, Chuck Berry, Ray Charles and Jerry Lee Lewis. The Beatles stood out initially by discovering unknown acts and obscure B-sides but even these were soon copied and became standard fare on Merseyside.

This was what pushed them into serious songwriting. It was the only guarantee of uniqueness. If you had your own material then you were set apart from the copyists.

It was this situation that prompted them into serious writing. Their goal was to come up with material that not only went down well with their audiences but which remained unique to their act. Paul has said that 'Like Dreamers Do' was one of the first of his own compositions that he tried at the Cavern. This implies that he wrote it for the Cavern audience but the Quarry Men were performing it as far back as 1958. What he probably meant was that it was one of the first songs from his back catalogue that he felt confident enough to slip into the Beatles regular set.

The early arrangement of the song, he thought was weak although "certain of the kids" at the Cavern liked it. When the Beatles came to audition for Decca on January 1st, 1962 it was one of three Lennon-McCartney songs that they included in a 15-song set (the others were 'Hello Little Girl' and 'Love Of The Loved').

By the time of their EMI audition nine months later, none of these songs were offered, all of them having been replaced by better material. Shortly afterwards they were offered to other artists, 'Like Dreamers Do' to The Applejacks, a Birmingham six-piece group with a female bassist, who reached number 20 with it in July 1964.

LIKE DREAMERS DO
Written:
Lennon/
McCartney
Length: 2' 35"
UK release:
Anthology 1
album, November
21, 1995
US release:
Anthology 1
album, November
21, 1995

HELLO LITTLE GIRL

John frequently referred to 'Hello Little Girl' as his earliest composition. Written in 1958, it became the first of his songs to be performed by the Quarry Men.

He credited its origin to the Cole Porter song 'It's De-Lovely', with its chorus of 'It's delightful, it's delicious, it's de-lovely', which was first sung by Bob Hope in the 1936 stage musical *Red, Hot and Blue* and was recorded in Britain by Carroll Gibbons and The Savoy Hotel Orpheans in 1938.

"That song always fascinated me for some reason or another," John said. "It was possibly connected to my mother. She used to sing that one. It's all very Freudian. So I made 'Hello Little Girl' out of it. It was supposed to be a Buddy Holly-style song."

There is no similarity between the two songs other than the device of repeating the title as a chorus. It may have been more the

The Beatles played 'Hello Little Girl' in their early sets before ditching it when they signed to EMI.

HELLO LITTLE GIRL

Written:	Lennon/McCartney
Length:	1'40"
UK release:	Anthology 1 album, November 21, 1995
US release:	Anthology 1 album, November 21, 1995

---

playful spirit of the song and, as with 'Please Please me', the association with his mother's musical interests. The imprint of Buddy Holly is more easily detectable. In its earliest incarnation the middle eight was apparently swiped wholesale from 'Maybe Baby'.

Just as Paul's early songs always bore the hallmark of optimism, John's bore the hallmark of pessimism. Paul assumed acceptance and love where John braced himself for rejection. In 'Hello Little Girl' he attempts to attract a girl's attention but she remains unaware of him. He sends her flowers but she is unmoved. He ends up lonely about to 'lose my mind'.

Recorded for the Decca audition in January 1962 'Hello Little Girl' was already off their set list by the time they signed for EMI later in the year. "It was then offered to Gerry and the Pacemakers," remembers Tony Bramwell. "It was considered as the follow up to 'How Do You Do It?'. They recorded a demo of it (included on *Gerry and the Pacemakers; The Best of the EMI Years*, 1992) but by that time Mitch Murray had come up with 'I Like It'."

The song was then offered to The Fourmost, another Liverpool group managed by Brian Epstein. After a Sunday concert in Blackpool where the two groups had appeared, John invited The Fourmost to his house to see the lyrics. The following morning they were sent a demo tape. "We had to record on the Wednesday and so we only had two days to record it," said bass guitarist Billy Hatton. "As a matter of fact, when we were recording, we were just learning the song as we went along."

The record was a hit after its release on August 23 and reached number 7 in the British charts. It was released in America on September 16.

YOU KNOW WHAT TO DO

A languid country-flavoured song written by George and recorded on June 3, 1964. Ringo had been taken ill that morning, on the verge of a tour, and so the studio time booked to record a fourteenth and final song for the *A Hard Day's Night* album had to be used to rehearse substitute drummer Jimmy Nicol. As a result only three new demos were recorded that day – Paul's 'It's For You' (later given to Cilla Black), John's 'No Reply' and this new song from George.

Being the youngest Beatle, George always had a hard time getting his ideas to be taken seriously. This was only the second song of his to be taped by the group (the first being 'Don't Bother Me') but it was never developed and, due to misfiling, it was lost for the next three decades. If it had been worked on by the group, it would surely have been a contender for *Beatles For Sale*.

Although it is undoubtedly a formula song with no deep revelation at the core it's interesting to note that George was just twelve weeks into his courtship of Pattie Boyd. Could he have written a song at the time about wanting to be with his girl 'every hour of the day' without having her in mind?

George wrote the under-rated 'You Know What To Do' a few weeks after he first met Pattie Boyd.

YOU KNOW WHAT TO DO

Written:	Harrison
Length:	1' 58"
UK release:	Anthology 1 album, November 21, 1995
US release:	Anthology 1 album, November 21, 1995

IF YOU'VE GOT TROUBLE

John and Paul never gave Ringo their best songs but neither did they only give him their worst. However, 'If You've Got Trouble' must rate as the worst one they ever expected him to sing. Melodically, it's uninspiring. Lyrically, it's embarrassing. It's hard to believe that the team that had just written 'Ticket To Ride' and ' You've Got To Hide Your Love Away' could come up with this. Recorded in one take, it sounds as though it was also composed in one take.

The theme of the song could be roughly summarised as 'If you think you've got problems - you should see mine!' The vitriol in the song sounds like John. Did it start out as a barbed attack on Cynthia, telling her to quit complaining about his abilities as a husband and a father and to be grateful for the luxuries afforded by the Beatles' new stardom?

An interview that year in the *Saturday Evening Post* conducted by Al Aronowitz suggests such a context for the song; "Their friends say that she (Cynthia) was in awe of John when they first met and she still is; a feeling, in fact, which has grown as his stardom rockets him further into the entertainment heavens, troubling her with the occasional thought that she might be left behind. When the Beatles are on tour, she often is left behind. 'Well, she certainly doesn't seem to mind spending the money I'm making," John says."

Intended for the *Help!* album, it was left to die after this session.

IF YOU'VE GOT TROUBLE
Written:
Lennon/
McCartney
Length: 2' 48"
UK release:
Anthology 2
album, March 18,
1996
US release:
Anthology 2
album, March 18,
1996

THAT MEANS A LOT

Written primarily by Paul, this was another song intended for *Help!* but which the Beatles were never able to record in what they considered to be a definitive version. In sessions on February 20th and March 30th, 1965 they attempted the song 24 times before finally abandoning it.

The band attempted to play 'That Means A Lot' 24 times in one 1965 session before finally giving it up.

The song takes the point of view of a third party looking in on a relationship, a device first used in 'She Loves You'. The shift in viewpoint opened up the possibility of writing in voices other than their own and expressing attitudes that were not necessarily their own.

"We found that we just couldn't sing it," summarised John some time later. "In fact, we made such a hash of it that we thought we'd better give it to someone who could do it well." That someone was P.J. Proby, an American singer who'd been invited to Britain by Brian Epstein in April 1964 to take part in a Beatles TV special, and who had become friendly with the group. Proby recorded 'That Means A Lot' and it made number 30 in the British charts in October 1965.

THAT MEANS A LOT
Written: Lennon/McCartney
Length: 2' 26"
UK release: Anthology 2 album, March 18, 1996
US release: Anthology 2 album, March 18, 1996

12-BAR ORIGINAL

Recorded between 'What Goes On' and 'I'm Looking Through You' in November 1965, was this song meant for *Rubber Soul*? Two takes were recorded, one was mixed, but neither was ever released.

It is one of the least typical Beatles' tracks and appears to be an attempt to mimic the Memphis soul sound. The obvious template is Booker T. & The MG's – keyboard player Booker T. Jones, drummer Al Jackson, bass player 'Duck' Dunn and guitarist Steve Cropper – the Stax Records session musicians who played behind such soul greats as Otis Redding, Sam and Dave, and Eddie Floyd. They had enjoyed a string of instrumental hits under their own name beginning with 'Green Onions' in 1962. '12-Bar Original', which is credited to all four Beatles, sounds like a pastiche of 'Green Onions' and its follow-up 'Jellybread' minus the distinctive keyboard playing.

The track was recorded at a point when the Beatles were striving for recognition as musicians and was also at a juncture in British pop when the heavier sounds of the Animals, Yardbirds, Kinks and Pretty Things were taking over from Tin Pan Alley.

All four Beatles shared credit for writing the atypical, Booker T & the MG's-like number '12-Bar Original'.

12-BAR ORIGINAL	
Written:	Harrison/Lennon/McCartney/Starr
Length:	2' 55"
UK release:	Anthology 2 album, March 18, 1996
US release:	Anthology 2 album, March 18, 1996

JUNK

Paul wrote 'Junk' while in India and first recorded it in May 1968 when all four Beatles met up at George's home on Claremont Drive, Esher, Surrey. It's this version, an acoustic demo with unfinished lyrics, that appears on *Anthology*. Paul hoped to complete it for inclusion on *Abbey Road* but instead recorded it for his first solo album, *McCartney*, which was released in April 1970.

The demo is nothing more than a rough sketch. An unfinished verse is repeated twice, he is still thinking up words for the chorus and the gaps are filled with humming and giggling.

It's impossible to determine the story because Paul's way of composing at the time was to fit interesting words to a tune he had hit upon, in this case words to do with a scrap yard and a junk shop. In the press release that went out with his solo album his only comment was; "Originally written in India, at Maharishi's camp, and completed bit by bit in London."

JUNK
Written: McCartney
Length: 2' 24"
UK release: Anthology 3 album, October 28, 1996
US release: Anthology 3 album, October 28, 1996

NOT GUILTY

Recorded during the White Album sessions in August 1968 George had already spent two months in the studio with only one of his songs – 'While My Guitar Gently Weeps' – having been picked up by the group. Over 100 takes and rehearsals of this song were produced between August 7 and August 12 but for some reason it wasn't included in the final line-up.

The song didn't surface until 1979 when a re-recorded version was used on the album *George Harrison*. Structurally the song remained the same, with the exception of the addition of the lines; 'not guilty for being on your street/ Getting underneath your feet'.

Around this time George explained the song as being about the problems that were beginning to affect him as a part of the Beatles in 1968: "Paul, John, Apple, Rishikesh, Indian friends etc." Written when he was starting to be regarded as the freaky, mystical Beatle he seems to be saying, "Don't blame me for getting you involved with freak culture. Hey, I'm not asking for too much. I just want to do my job and get a bit of respect."

It's hard not to see such lines as, 'I'm not trying to be smart/ I only want what I can get' as a bitter comment on his inability to increase his presence within the group and become regarded as a songwriting equal to John and Paul.

Maybe that's why it didn't get on the album.

George expressed his resentment at seeing his songwriting relegated behind that of Paul and John in the bitter 'Not Guilty'.

NOT GUILTY
Written: Harrison
Length: 3' 22"
UK release:
Anthology 3
album, October
28, 1996
US release:
Anthology 3
album, October
28, 1996

WHAT'S THE NEW MARY JANE

"This was a thing I wrote half with our electronic genius Alex," said John in 1969. "It was called 'What A Shame Mary Jane Had A Pain At The Party' and it was meant for *The Beatles* album."

Written in India when the Greek-born John Alexis Mardas paid a visit, it was demoed at George's Esher home in May 1968. At this stage it was a little over two and a half minutes long and as the Beatles improvised towards the end of the track one of them shouted, "Ooh. What's the news?…What are you saying? What a shame Mary Jane had a pain at the party. What's the new Mary Jane…Oh, my God! Mary! Mary!" This gave rise to the unusual title.

The studio version, recorded by John and George with help from Yoko and Mal Evans, went on for over six minutes with a two-minute 'freak out' before the final verse. The lyric remained the same as demoed in May except for the line 'He cooking such groovy spaghetti' which came out, whether by accident or creative play, as 'He groovy such cooking spaghetti'.

The syntax of the lyric is unorthodox. There is a deliberate use of wrong tenses and wrong words which suggest that John may have been imitating the way that Indians often speak English when it is their second language. The story told is either deliberate or a coded putdown of someone in Maharishi's circle. Significantly, John had been recording 'Sexy Sadie' the day before.

At the end of the recording John can be heard saying, "Let's hear it before we get taken away". A year later he planned to have it released as a B side to 'You Know My Name (Look Up The Number)' as a Plastic Ono Band single but it was pulled at the last minute. "It was real madness," said John describing the track in 1969. "I'd like to do it again."

WHAT'S THE NEW MARY JANE
Written:
Lennon/
McCartney
Length: 6' 12"
UK release:
Anthology 3
album, October
28, 1996
US release:
Anthology 3
album, October
28, 1996

STEP INSIDE LOVE

Cilla Black, real name Priscilla White, was a Liverpool typist signed by Brian Epstein and given a contract with Parlophone. Her first single, released in February 1963, was 'Love Of The Loved', an old Quarry Men song written by Paul and used by the Beatles at their Decca Records audition. Paul turned up for the recording.

In 1964 he wrote 'It's For You' for her and then in 1968, after hearing that she was to front her own BBC TV series, he offered to write the theme song for her. Entertainment shows of the time were traditionally book-ended by big band numbers but Cilla wanted to change that.

"Paul understood what I felt," she said. "He said to me: 'I know what they're doing. They're sending you these Billy Cotton Band-type of numbers and that's not you. You're the kind of person that should invite people into your house. You should have a song that that starts off very quietly and then builds up.'"

Paul did a demo of 'Step Inside Love' at his home in Cavendish Avenue and double tracked it with his own voice. "All he had given us was one verse and a chorus with him playing on guitar," remembers director and producer Michael Hurll. "We played it that way for the first couple of weeks and then decided that we needed a second

---

STEP INSIDE LOVE

Written:	Lennon/McCartney
Length:	2' 30"
UK release:	Anthology 3 album, October 28, 1996
US release:	Anthology 3 album, October 28, 1996

Paul wrote 'Step Inside Love' as the theme tune for Cilla Black's 1968 BBC TV show.

verse. Paul came over to the BBC Theatre in Shepherd's Bush and sat with me and Cilla and worked on a second verse. It started off with the line 'You look tired love' because Cilla was tired after a lot of rehearsing and most of what he wrote related to what was going on that day."

The version of the song included on *Anthology* was captured in September 1968 while the Beatles were waiting to record 'I Will'. Paul begins with the chorus and slips straight into the second verse which he forgets, singing 'kiss me goodnight' instead of 'love me tonight', leaving a line out and concluding with the last line of what should have been the third verse.

'Step Inside Love' became a Top Ten hit for Cilla in Britain, was released in America in May and earned her a ban in South Africa where it was considered to be a play on a prostitute's invitation. It could have been worse. Tony Bramwell remembers that Paul's initial idea was 'Come Inside Love'.

"I quite like the song," said Paul. "It was just a welcoming song for Cilla. It was very cabaret. It suited her voice."

LOS PARANOIAS

This was nothing more than an extended studio joke initiated by Paul when, at the end of his bossa nova version of 'Step Inside Love' he announced in the voice of an MC, 'Joe Prairie and the Prairie Wall Flyers'. John responded with 'Los Paranoias' which was enough to get Paul improvising a South American spoof about Los Paranoias.

The likely inspiration was the Paraguayan group Trio Los Paraguayas led by Luis Alberto Del Parana who appeared in variety shows on British TV during the 1950s with their 'Latin American rhythms' and released a *Best Of* album in 1957.

'Los Paranoias' was no more than a Beatles' studio in-joke.

LOS PARANOIAS
Written: Lennon/McCartney
Length: Snippet at the end of 'Step Inside Love'
UK release: Anthology 3 album, October 28, 1996
US release: Anthology 3 album, October 28, 1996

TEDDY BOY

"Another song started in India," announced Paul in 1970 when 'Teddy Boy' was included on his first solo album. "It was recorded for the *Get Back* album but later not used." It was started during one of the Maharishi's lectures at Rishikesh when Paul turned to John and sang the first line in his ear and was then finished in Scotland and London.

Strictly speaking, it was never 'recorded' by the Beatles because there was no final take, no mixing and in January 1969 Paul had still not completed the lyric. What is presented on *Anthology* is a rough sketch of a song offered by Paul in the hopes that John, George and Ringo would like it. The atmosphere is so informal that Paul laughs in parts, whistles over the unwritten patches and John can be clearly heard talking to others in the studio as he played along.

This inconsequential tale of a boy called Ted who is told to be good by his mother is not one that would have warmed John's heart. He once referred to Paul's story songs as being about, "Boring people doing boring things". This is probably why, as the song ended during this session, John picked up the rhythm on his guitar and turned it into a clunky square-dance song; 'Take your partners do-si-do/ Hold them tight and don't let go'. That was his none-too-subtle comment about where 'Teddy Boy' fitted into sixties rock culture.

TEDDY BOY
Written:
McCartney
Length: 3' 18"
UK release:
Anthology 3
album, October
28, 1996
US release:
Anthology 3
album, October
28, 1996

177

ALL THINGS
MUST PASS

In November 1968, after finishing up his work on the *White Album*, George had gone to Woodstock to stay with Bob Dylan. Here he also spent time with The Band, Dylan's former backing group, who had just recorded *Music From Big Pink*.

This album was seen at the time as a reaction against the excesses of psychedelia and a return to the mainstream of American music. The bluntness of the group's name and the rustic simplicity of their publicity photographs suggested a swing away from surrealism and a return to the roots of American culture.

Their music was particularly appealing to seasoned musicians weary of the demands of fan hysteria. It was instrumental in the break-up of Cream, for example. "I got the tapes of *Music From Big Pink* and I thought this is what I want to play – not extended solos and maestro bullshit but just good, funky songs," he explained in 1974.

George's song 'All Things Must Pass', which he played during Beatles recording sessions in January 1969 and then recorded alone on February 25th, was an attempt to capture the feeling that the

---

ALL THINGS MUST PASS

Written:	Harrison
Length:	3' 05"
UK release:	Anthology 3 album, October 28, 1996
US release:	Anthology 3 album, October 28, 1996

George based 'All Things Must Pass' on a Timothy Leary poem but it failed to make it onto a Beatles album.

Band had captured on their single 'The Weight'. In fact, when George first played it through to John and Paul he openly enthused about the Band and their music.

The lyric was based on a poem from Timothy Leary's book *Psychedelic Prayers After The Tao Te Ching* (Poets Press, New York, 1966). The poem was a 'translation from English to psychedelese' of part of the 23rd chapter of the Tao that Leary had titled 'All Things Pass'; *'All things pass/ A sunrise does not last all morning/ All things pass/ A cloudburst does not last all day...'* As George was to admit; "I remembered one of these prayers and it gave me the idea for this thing."

Despite George's frequent references to the song while the others were recording it wasn't considered for either *Let It Be* or *Abbey Road*. Instead, it became the title track of his debut solo album in December 1970 which reached number 4 in the British album charts and topped the American charts.

COME AND GET IT

Apple Films, which was being run by Denis O'Dell, were planning a film of Terry Southern's 1958 novel *The Magic Christian* and O'Dell asked Paul to do the music. Paul agreed, reluctantly it now seems, and with a shooting script in hand began to write.

He started with a song to be used over a scene where Sir Guy Grand, the world's richest man, (played by Peter Sellers), throws banknotes into a vat of filth and gets pleasure from seeing respectable people wallowing in slime in the hopes of grabbing some free cash. The idea came to him late at night while at Cavendish Avenue and he came downstairs and taped it in a whisper so as not to wake Linda. When he played it back the next day he believed that he had come up with "a very catchy song".

On July 5th, 1969 one of the Apple label signings, a group called The Iveys, gave an interview to *Disc & Music Echo* in which they complained of being neglected by the Beatles. Three weeks later Paul contacted the group and on July 29th he met them at their home and offered them 'Come And Get It' which he'd recorded alone with engineer Phil MacDonald five days previously at Abbey Road. He also suggested that they might make other contributions to the film

---

COME AND GET IT

Written:	McCartney
Length:	2' 29"
UK release:	Anthology 3 album, October 28, 1996
US release:	Anthology 3 album, October 28, 1996

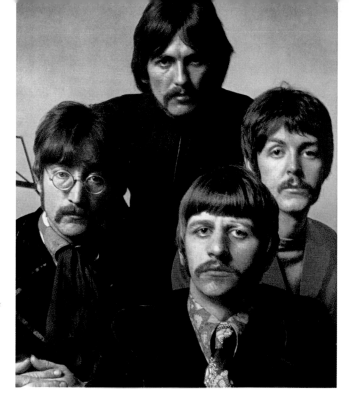

Paul denied that 'Come And Get It' detailed the Beatles' intra-band travails: "It was just a straightforward pop song," he claimed.

soundtrack as he was trying to put his energies into recording the *Abbey Road* album.

Paul produced the group on August 2nd, choosing Tom Evans to do the lead vocal and encouraging them to stick to the simplicity of his demo on which he'd played only piano, drums, bass and maracas. He told them that if they did it right he could guarantee them a hit and if they didn't do it right then he'd keep it for a Beatles single. "That challenge really made us work hard," said Evans.

By the time 'Come And Get It ' came out The Iveys were Badfinger (after John's 'Badfinger Boogie'). The single reached the top five and the group could no longer say they were neglected. The soundtrack to *The Magic Christian* contained three Badfinger songs and in a move to capitalize on this they titled their next album *Magic Christian Music*.

Asked whether 'Come And Get It' was a veiled message to those squabbling over the Beatles fortune in 1968, Paul said; "It was just a straightforward pop song with all the old innuendoes. Come and get what?"

CHRONOLOGY

1967

Jan 1 – April 2
Recording continues on *Sgt Pepper's Lonely Hearts Club Band*

April 3
Paul flies to San Francisco

June 1
Sgt Pepper's Lonely Hearts Club Band is released in America

June 16
Paul becomes the first Beatle to confess to having taken LSD, in a *Life* cover story

June 25
Our World television programme in which the Beatles sing the specially composed 'All You Need Is Love'.

July 24
Beatles sign petition for the legalization of cannabis which is published in the London *Times*

Aug 1
George and Pattie fly to Los Angeles and later on to San Francisco where they visit the Haight Ashbury district

Aug 24
All four Beatles attend a lecture given by the Maharishi Mahesh Yogi at the Hilton Hotel in London's Park Lane

Aug 25
At the personal invitation of the Maharishi the Beatles travel to Bangor, North Wales, for a summer school in Transcendental Meditation

Aug 27
Brian Epstein dies

Sept 11 – 24
Magical Mystery Tour is filmed

Sept 22
Beatles make the cover of *Time* magazine

Oct 18
World premiere of *How I Won The War*, starring John Lennon

Dec 5
Apple Boutique opens at 94 Baker Street, London W1

Dec 25
Paul announces his engagement to Jane Asher

Dec 26
Magical Mystery Tour premiered on British television (BBC)

1968

Feb 15
John, Cynthia, George and Pattie fly out to India to join the Maharishi at his ashram in Rishikesh where they will study meditation

Feb 19
Paul, Jane, Ringo and Maureen join the rest of the Beatles in India

May 15
John and Paul travel to New York to announce the formation of Apple. Paul is reunited with Linda Eastman

May
John begins his affair with Yoko Ono

May 30
Beatles demo the songs written during their stay in India

May 31 – Oct 14
Recording *The Beatles*, better known as The White Album

June 20 – 24
Paul is in Los Angeles on business and again meets up with Linda Eastman

July 20
Jane Asher announces that her engagement to Paul is off

July 31
The Apple Boutique is closed down

Oct 16
George goes to California to produce Apple artist Jackie Lomax

Oct 18
John and Yoko arrested on a charge of drug possession

Nov 8
Divorce granted to John and Cynthia

Nov 10
John puts his Weybridge home on the market

1969

Jan 2
Filming begins in Twickenham for what will eventually become the documentary *Let It Be*

Feb 2
Yoko Ono and Tony Cox divorce

Feb 10
George temporarily leaves the group after disagreements with John and Paul

Mar 12
Paul marries Linda Eastman at Marylebone Registry Office in London

Mar 20
John marries Yoko Ono in Gibraltar

Mar 25 – 31
John and Yoko organize their first 'bed-in' at the Amsterdam Hilton

Mar 28
It is announced that ATV are poised to buy Northern Songs

May 26 – June 2
John and Yoko arrange a bed-in at the Queen Elizabeth Hotel in Montreal

July 1
Work begins in earnest on the *Abbey Road*

album

Aug 8   Iain MacMillan shoots the celebrated cover photo of the four Beatles walking across Abbey Road

Aug 11   John and Yoko move to Tittenhurst Park, Sunningdale, Ascot

Aug 20   The last day on which all four Beatles would be together in a recording studio

Aug 31   John, George and Ringo see Bob Dylan perform at the Isle of Wight festival

Sept 13   The Plastic Ono band (John, Yoko, Eric Clapton, Klaus Voorman and Alan White) makes its live debut in Toronto

Nov 25   John returns his MBE to Buckingham Palace

1970

Jan 4   The final taping of *Let It Be*

Apr 10   Paul announces that he has left the Beatles due to "personal, business and musical differences"

May – Aug   Battles over the ownership of Northern Songs and involvement of Allen Klein continue

Aug 4   Apple's press office closes down

Dec 31   Paul files a suit against The Beatles and Co to dissolve the partnership

DISCOGRAPHY 1967-70

UK RELEASES

SINGLES

'Strawberry Fields Forever'/'Penny Lane', February 17, 1967, Parlophone R 5570.

'All You Need Is Love'/'Baby, You're A Rich Man', July 7, 1967, Parlophone R 5620

'Hello, Goodbye'/'I Am The Walrus', November 24, 1967, Parlophone R 5655.

'Lady Madonna'/'The Inner Light', March 15, 1968, Parlophone R 5675.

'Hey Jude'/'Revolution', August 30, 1968, Apple [Parlophone] R 5722.

'Get Back'/'Don't Let Me Down', April 11, 1969, Apple [Parlophone] R 5777.

'The Ballad Of John And Yoko'/'Old Brown Shoe', May 30, 1969, Apple [Parlophone] R 5786.

'Something'/'Come Together', October 31, 1969, Apple [Parlophone] R 5814.

'Let It Be'/'You Know My Name (Look Up The Number)', March 6, 1970, Apple [Parlophone] R 5833.

'Free As A Bird'/'I Saw Her Standing There'/'This Boy'/'Christmas Time (Is Here Again)', December 4 1995, Apple [Parlophone] CDR 6422

'Real Love'/'Baby's In Black'/'Yellow Submarine'/'Here, There And Everywhere', March 4, 1996, Apple [Parlophone] CDR 6425

EPS

Magical Mystery Tour, December 8, 1967, Parlophone MMT-1 (mono), SMMT-1 (stereo) – 'Magical Mystery Tour'; 'Your Mother Should Know'/'I Am The Walrus'; 'The Fool On The Hill'; 'Flying'/'Blue Jay Way'.

ALBUMS

Sgt Pepper's Lonely Hearts Club Band, June 1, 1967, Parlophone PMC 7017 (mono), PCS 7027 (stereo) – 'Sgt Pepper's Lonely Hearts Club Band'; 'With A Little Help From My Friends'; 'Lucy In The Sky With Diamonds'; 'Getting Better'; 'Fixing A Hole'; 'She's Leaving Home'; 'Being For The Benefit Of Mr Kite!'/'Within You Without You'; 'When I'm Sixty Four'; 'Lovely Rita'; 'Good Morning Good Morning'; 'Sgt Pepper's Lonely Hearts Club Band (Reprise)'; 'A Day In The Life'.

The Beatles, November 22, 1968, Apple [Parlophone] PMC 7067-7068 (mono), PCS 7067-7068 (stereo) – 'Back In The USSR'; 'Dear Prudence'; 'Glass Onion'; 'Ob-La-Di, Ob-La-Da'; 'Wild Honey Pie'; 'The Continuing Story Of Bungalow Bill'; 'While My Guitar Gently Weeps'; 'Happiness Is A Warm Gun'/'Martha My Dear'; 'I'm So Tired'; 'Blackbird'; 'Piggies'; 'Rocky Raccoon'; 'Don't Pass Me By'; 'Why Don't We Do It In The Road'; 'I Will'; 'Julia'/'Birthday'; 'Yer Blues'; 'Mother Nature's Son'; 'Everybody's Got Something To Hide Except Me And My Monkey'; 'Sexy Sadie'; 'Helter Skelter'; 'Long Long Long'/'Revolution 1'; 'Honey Pie'; 'Savoy Truffle'; 'Cry Baby Cry'; 'Revolution 9'; 'Good Night'.

Yellow Submarine, January 17, 1969, Apple [Parlophone] PMC 7070 (mono), PCS 7070 (stereo) – 'Yellow Submarine'; 'Only A Northern Song'; 'All Together Now'; 'Hey Bulldog'; 'It's All Too Much'; 'All You Need Is Love'/ [Seven soundtrack instrumental cuts by the George Martin Orchestra].

Abbey Road, September 26, 1969, Apple [Parlophone] PCS 7088 (stereo only) – 'Come Together'; 'Something'; 'Maxwell's Silver Hammer'; 'Oh! Darling'; 'Octopus's Garden'; 'I Want You (She's So Heavy)'/'Here Comes The Sun'; 'Because'; 'You Never Give Me Your Money'; 'Sun King'/'Mean Mr Mustard'; 'Polythene Pam'/'She Came In Through The Bathroom Window'; 'Golden Slumbers'/'Carry That Weight'; 'The End'; Her Majesty'.

Let It Be, May 8, 1970, Apple [Parlophone] PCS 7096 (stereo only) – 'Two Of Us'; 'Dig A Pony'; 'Across The Universe'; 'I Me Mine'; 'Dig It'; 'Let It Be'; 'Maggie Mae'/'I've Got A Feeling'; 'The One After 909'; 'The Long And Winding Road'; 'For You Blue'; 'Get Back'.

Live At The BBC, November 30, 1994, Apple [Parlophone] CDPCSP 726 TC (mono) – 'From Us To You'; 'I Got A Woman'; 'Too Much Monkey Business'; 'Keep Your Hands Off My Baby'; 'I'll Be On My Way'; 'Young Blood'; 'A Shot Of Rhythm And Blues'; 'Sure To Fall (In Love With You)'; 'Some Other Guy'; 'Thank You Girl'; 'Baby It's You'; 'That's All Right (Mama)'; 'Carol'; 'Soldier Of Love'; 'Clarabella'; 'I'm Gonna Sit Right Down And Cry (Over You)'; 'Crying, Waiting, Hoping'; 'You Really Got A Hold On Me'; 'To Know Her Is To Love Her'; 'A Taste Of Honey'; 'Long Tall Sally'; 'I Saw Her Standing There'; 'The Honeymoon Song'; 'Johnny B Goode'; 'Memphis, Tennessee'; 'Lucille'; 'Can't Buy Me Love'; 'Till There Was You'; 'A Hard Day's Night'; 'I Wanna Be Your Man'; 'Roll Over Beethoven'; 'Things We Said Today'; 'She's A Woman'; 'Sweet Little Sixteen'; 'Lonesome Tears In My Eyes'; 'Nothin' Shakin''; 'The Hippy Hippy Shake'; 'Glad All Over'; 'I Just Don't Understand'; 'So How Come (No One Loves Me)'; 'I Feel Fine'; 'I'm A Loser'; 'Everybody's Trying To Be My Baby'; 'Rock And Roll Music'; 'Ticket To Ride'; 'Dizzy Miss Lizzy'; 'Kansas City/'Hey! Hey! Hey!'; 'Matchbox'; 'I Forgot To Remember To Forget'; 'I Got To Find My Baby'; 'Ooh! My Soul'; 'Don't Ever Change'; 'Slow Down'; 'Honey Don't'; Love Me Do'.

Anthology 1, November 21, 1995, Apple [Parlophone] CDPCSP 727 – 'Free As A Bird'; 'That'll Be The Day'; 'In Spite Of All The Danger'; 'Hallelujah, I Love Her So'; 'You'll Be Mine'; 'Cayenne'; 'My Bonnie'; 'Ain't She Sweet'; 'Cry For A Shadow'; 'Searchin''; 'Three Cool Cats'; 'The Sheik Of Araby'; 'Like Dreamers Do'; 'Hello Little Girl'; 'Besame Mucho'; 'Love Me Do'; 'How Do You Do It'; 'Please Please Me'; 'One After 909'; 'Lend Me Your Comb'; 'I'll Get You'; 'I Saw Her Standing There'; 'From Me To You'; 'Money (That's What I Want)'; 'You Really Got A Hold On Me'; 'Roll Over Beethoven'; 'She Loves You'; 'Till There Was You'; 'Twist And Shout'; 'This Boy'; 'I Want To Hold Your Hand'; 'Moonlight Bay'; 'Can't Buy Me Love'; 'All My Loving'; 'You Can't Do That'; 'And I Love Her'; 'A Hard Day's Night'; 'I Wanna Be Your Man'; 'Long Tall Sally'; 'Boys'; 'Shout'; 'I'll Be Back', 'You Know What To Do'; 'No Reply' (Demo); 'Mr Moonlight'; 'Leave My Kitten Alone'; 'No Reply'; 'Eight Days A Week'; 'Kansas City'/'Hey! Hey! Hey!'.

Anthology 2, March 18, 1996, Apple [Parlophone] CDPCSP 728 – 'Real Love'; 'Yes It Is'; 'I'm Down'; 'You've Got To Hide Your Love Away'; 'If You've Got Trouble'; 'That Means A Lot'; 'Yesterday'; 'It's Only Love'; 'I Feel Fine'; 'Ticket To Ride'; 'Yesterday'; 'Help!'; 'Everybody's Trying To Be My Baby'; 'Norwegian Wood (This Bird Has Flown)'; 'I'm Looking Through You'; '12-Bar Original'; 'Tomorrow Never Knows'; 'Got To Get You Into

My Life'; 'And Your Bird Can Sing'; 'Taxman'; 'Eleanor Rigby' (Strings Only); 'I'm Only Sleeping' (rehearsal); 'I'm Only Sleeping' (take 1); 'Rock And Roll Music'; 'She's A Woman'; 'Strawberry Fields Forever' (Demo); 'Strawberry Fields Forever' (Take 1); 'Strawberry Fields Forever' (Take 7); 'Penny Lane'; 'A Day In The Life'; 'Good Morning Good Morning'; 'Only A Northern Song'; ' Being For The Benefit Of Mr Kite! (Takes 1 and 2); 'Being For The Benefit Of Mr Kite!' (Take 7); 'Lucy In The Sky With Diamonds', 'Within You Without You' (Instrumental); 'Sgt Pepper's Lonely Hearts Club Band' (Reprise); 'You Know My Name (Look Up The Number); 'I Am The Walrus'; 'The Fool On The Hill' (Demo); 'Your Mother Should Know'; 'The Fool On The Hill' (Take 4); 'Hello, Goodbye'; 'Lady Madonna'; 'Across The Universe'.

Anthology 3, October 28, 1996, Apple [Parlophone] CDPCSP 729 – 'A Beginning'; 'Happiness Is A Warm Gun'; 'Helter Skelter'; 'Mean Mr Mustard'; 'Polythene Pam'; 'Glass Onion'; 'Junk'; 'Piggies'; 'Honey Pie'; 'Don't Pass Me By'; 'Ob-La-Di, Ob-La-Da'; 'Good Night'; 'Cry Baby Cry'; 'Blackbird'; 'Sexy Sadie'; 'While My Guitar Gently Weeps'; 'Hey Jude'; 'Not Guilty'; 'Mother Nature's Son'; 'Glass Onion'; 'Rocky Raccoon'; 'What's The New Mary Jane'; 'Step Inside Love'/'Los Paranoias'; 'I'm So Tired'; 'I Will'; 'Why Don't We Do It In The Road'; 'Julia'; 'I've Got A Feeling'; 'She Came In Through The Bathroom Window'; 'Dig A Pony'; 'Two Of Us'; 'For You Blue'; 'Teddy Boy'; 'Rip It Up'/ 'Shake, Rattle and Roll'/ 'Blue Suede Shoes'; 'The Long And Winding Road'; 'Oh! Darling'; 'All Things Must Pass'; 'Mailman, Bring Me No More Blues'; 'Get Back'; 'Old Brown Shoe'; ' Octopus's Garden'; 'Maxwell's Silver Hammer'; 'Something';

'Come Together'; 'Come And Get It'; 'Ain't She Sweet'; 'Because'; 'Let It Be'; 'I Me Mine'; 'The End'.

Yellow Submarine Songtrack, September 13, 1999, Apple [Parlophone] 521 4812 – 'Yellow Submarine'; 'Hey Bulldog'; 'Eleanor Rigby'; 'Love You To'; 'All Together Now'; 'Lucy In The Sky With Diamonds'; 'Think For Yourself'; 'Sgt. Pepper's Lonely Hearts Club Band'; 'With A Little Help From My Friends'; 'Baby You're A Rich Man'; 'Only A Northern Song'; 'All You Need Is Love'; 'When I'm Sixty Four'; 'Nowhere Man'; 'It's All Too Much'.

1, November 13, 2000, Apple [Parlophone] 529 9702 – 'Love Me Do'; 'From Me To You'; 'She Loves You'; 'I Want To Hold Your Hand'; 'Can't Buy Me Love'; 'A Hard Day's Night'; 'I Feel Fine'; 'Eight Days A Week'; 'Ticket To Ride'; 'Help!'; 'Yesterday'; 'Day Tripper'; 'We Can Work It Out'; 'Paperback Writer'; 'Yellow Submarine'; 'Eleanor Rigby'; 'Penny Lane'; 'All You Need Is Love'; 'Hello, Goodbye'; 'Lady Madonna'; 'Hey Jude'; 'Get Back'; 'The Ballad Of John And Yoko'; 'Something'; 'Come Together'; 'Let It Be'; 'The Long and Winding Road'.

Let It Be… Naked, November 17, 2003, Aapple [Parlophone] 595 7132 - 'Get Back'; 'Dig A Pony'; 'For You Blue'; 'The Long And Winding Road'; 'Two Of Us'; 'I've Got A Feeling'; 'One After 909'; 'Don't Let Me Down'; 'I Me Mine'; 'Across The Universe'; 'Let It Be'.

US RELEASES

SINGLES

'Strawberry Fields Forever'/'Penny Lane', February 13, 1967, Capitol 5810.

'All You Need Is Love'/'Baby, You're A Rich Man', 17 July 1967, Capitol 5964.

'Lady Madonna'/'The Inner Light', March 18, 1968, Apple [Capitol] 2138.

'Hey Jude'/'Revolution', August 26, 1968, Apple [Capitol] 2276.

'Get Back'/'Don't Let Me Down', May 5, 1969, Apple [Capitol] 2490.

'The Ballad Of John And Yoko'/'Old Brown Shoe', June 4, 1969. Apple [Capitol] 2531.

'Something'/'Come Together', October 6, 1969, Apple [Capitol] 2654.

'Let It Be'/'You Know My Name (Look Up The Number)', March 11, 1970, Apple [Capitol] 2764.

'The Long And Winding Road'/'For You Blue', May 11, 1970, Apple [Capitol] 2832.

'Free As A Bird'/'I Saw Her Standing There'/'This Boy'/'Christmas Time (Is Here Again)', December 4, 1995, Apple [Capitol] C2 7243 8 584 972

'Real Love'/'Baby's In Black'/'Yellow Submarine'/ Here, There And Everywhere', March 4, 1996, Apple [Capitol] C2 7243 8 585 442

ALBUMS

Sgt Pepper's Lonely Hearts Club Band, June 2, 1967, Capitol MAS-2653 (mono), SMAS-2653 (stereo) – tracks as UK release

Magical Mystery Tour, November 27, 1967, Capitol MAL-2835 (mono), SMAL-2835 (stereo) – 'Magical Mystery Tour'; 'The Fool On The Hill'; 'Flying'; 'Blue Jay Way'; 'Your Mother Should

Know'; 'I Am The Walrus'/'Hello, Goodbye'; 'Strawberry Fields Forever'; 'Penny Lane'; 'Baby, You're A Rich Man'; 'All You Need Is Love'.

The Beatles, November 25, 1968, Apple [Capitol] SWBO-101 (stereo) – tracks as UK release

Yellow Submarine, January 13, 1969, Apple [Capitol] SW-153 (stereo) – tracks as UK release

Abbey Road, October 1, 1969, Apple [Capitol] SO-383 (stereo) – tracks as UK release

Hey Jude, February 26, 1970, Apple [Capitol] SW-385 (stereo) – 'Can't Buy Me Love'; 'I Should Have Known Better'; 'Paperback Writer'; 'Rain'; 'Lady Madonna'; 'Revolution'/ 'Hey Jude'; 'Old Brown Shoe'; 'Don't Let Me Down'; 'The Ballad Of John And Yoko'.

Let It Be, May 18, 1970, Apple [Capitol] AR-34001 (stereo) – tracks as UK release

Live At The BBC, November 30, 1994, Apple [Capitol] (mono) – tracks as UK release

Anthology 1, November 21, 1995, Apple [Capitol] – tracks as UK release

Anthology 2, March 18, 1996, Apple [Capitol] – tracks as UK release

Anthology 3, October 28, 1996, Apple [Capitol] – tracks as UK release

Yellow Submarine Songtrack, September 14, 1999, Apple [Capitol] – tracks as UK release

1, November 14, 2000, Apple [Capitol] – tracks as UK release

Let It Be… Naked, November 17, 2003, Apple [Capitol] – tracks as UK release

BIBLIOGRAPHY

BOOKS ABOUT THE BEATLES

Bacon, David and Maslov, Norman. *The Beatles' England*. Columbus Books, London ,1982; 910 Books, San Francisco, 1982.

Baird, Julia. *John Lennon My Brother*. Grafton, London, 1988.

Beatles, The, Anthology, Cassell & Co., London, 2000.

Beatles, The, The Beatles Lyrics. MacDonald, London, 1969.

Bedford, Carol. *Waiting For The Beatles*, Blandford Press, Newron Abbot, 1984.

Braun, Michael. *Love Me Do*. Penguin, London, 1964.

Brown, Peter. *The Love You Make*. MacMillan, London,1983.

Coleman, Ray. *Lennon*. McGraw Hill, New York, 1984.

Dalton, David and Cott, Jonathan. *The Beatles Get Back*. Apple, London, 1969.

Davies, Hunter. *The Beatles*. Heinemann, London 1968.

Elson, Howard. *McCartney: Songwriter*. W.H.Allen, London, 1986.

Evans, Mike (ed), *The Beatles Literary Anthology*, Plexus, London, 2004.

Freeman, Robert. *The Beatles: A Private View*. Pyramid, London, 1992.

Fulpen, H.V. *The Beatles: An Illustrated Diary*. Plexus, London, 1982.

Giuliano, Geoffrey. *Blackbird*. Smith Gryphon, London, 1991.

Goldman, Albert. *The Lives Of John Lennon*. Bantam Press, London, New York.

Gottfridsson, Hans. *The Beatles from Cavern to Star Club*. Premium Publishing, Stockholm, 1997.

Harrison, George. *I Me Mine*. W.H.Allen, London, 1980.

Harry, Bill (Editor). *Mersey Beat; The Beginnings Of The Beatles*. Columbus Books, London, 1977.

The Ultimate Beatles Encyclopedia. Virgin, London, 1992.

Henke, James, *Lennon Legend,* Weidenfeld & Nicolson, London, 2003.

Lennon, Cynthia. *A Twist Of Lennon*. W.H. Allen, London 1978.

Lennon, John. *In His Own Write*. Jonathan Cape, London,1964.

Lewisohn, Mark. *The Complete Beatles Recording Sessions*. Hamlyn, London, 1988.

The Complete Beatles Chronicle. Pyramid, London, 1992.

McCabe, Peter and Schonfeld, Robert. *Apple To The Core*. Sphere Books, London, 1972.

McCartney, Mike. *Thank U Very Much*. Weidenfeld & Nicolson, London, 1982.

Mellers, Wilfrid. *Twilight Of The Gods*. Schirmer Books, New York, 1973.

Miles, Barry. *Paul McCartney: Many Years from Now*. Secker & Warburg, London, 1997.

Miles, Barry, *The Beatles: A Diary*, Omnibus Press, London, 2002.

Norman, Philip. *Shout*, Elm Tree, London, 1981.

Pedler, Dominic, *The Songwriting Secrets Of The Beatles*, Omnibus Press, London, 2003.

Quantick, David, *Revolution: The Making of the Beatles' White Album*, Unanimous, London, 2002.

Rolling Stone magazine. *The Ballad Of John and Yoko*. Michael Joseph, London, 1982.

Salewicz, Chris. *McCartney: The Biography*. MacDonald, London, 1986.

Schafiner, Nicholas. *The Beatles Forever*. MSF Books, New York, 1978.

Schultheiss, Tom. *A Day In The Life*. Pierian Press, Ann Arbor, 1980.

Sheff, David. *The Playboy Interviews with John Lennon and Yoko Ono*. New English Library, London, 1981; Playboy Press, Chicago, 1981.

Shepherd, Billy. The *True Story of the Beatles*. Beat Publications, London, 1964.

Shotton, Pete. *John Lennon In My Life*. Stein & Day, New York, 1983.

Stuart Ryan. David, *John Lennon's Secret*, Kozmik Press Center, New York, 1982.

Taylor, Alistair. *Yesterday*. Sidgwick and Jackson, London; Pioneer Books, Las Vegas, 1989.

Wenner, Jann. *Lennon Remembers*. Straight Arrow Books, San Francisco, 1971.

Wiener, Jon. *Come Together: John Lennon In His Time*. Faber & Faber, London, 1984; Random House, New York, 1984

GENERAL BOOKS

Anthony, Gene. *Summer Of Love*. Celestial Arts, Berkeley, 1980.

Buglioso, Vincent. *Helter Skelter*. Bantam, New York, 1974.

Fein, Art. *The LA Musical History Tour*. Faber and Faber, Boston, 1990.

Gaines, Steven. *Heroes and Villains*. MacMillian, London, 1986; New American Library, New York, 1986.

Gibran, Kahlil. *Sand and Foam*, 1927.

Gillett, Charlie. *The Sound Of The City*. Sphere Books, London, 1970.

Goodman, Pete. *The Rolling Stones: Our Own Story*. Bantam, New York, 1965.

Guinness Book of Rock Stars. Guinness, London, 1989.

Hotchner, A.E. *Blown Away*. Simon and Schuster, London, 1990.

Leary, Timothy. *Flashbacks*. Heinemann, London, 1983.

Maharishi Mahesh Yogi,. *The Science of Being and the Art of Living*. International SRM Publications, London, 1963.

Mascaró, Juan. *Lamps of Fire,* Methuen, London 1958.

Marsh, Dave. *The Heart of Rock and Roll*. Penguin, London, 1989; New American Library, New York, 1989

Oldham, Andrew Loog, *Stoned*, Secker & Warburg, London, 2000.

Smith, Joe. *Off The Record*. Sidgwick and Jackson, London, 1989.

Stein, Jean. *Edie*. Jonathan Cape, London, 1982.

Turner, John M. *A Dictionary of Circus Biography* (unpublished).

White, Charles. *Little Richard*. Pan, London, 1984.

Wolfe, Tom. *The Electric Kool-Aid Acid Test*. Bantam, New York, 1968.

Worth, Fred and Tamerius, Steve. *Elvis: His Life from A-Z*. Contemporary Books, New York, 1988.

Wyman, Bill. *Stone Alone*. Viking, London, 1990

INDEX

Numbers in italics refer to captions

ACKNOWLEDGEMENTS

For interviews carried out specifically for this book I thank: Al Aronowitz, Diane Ashley, Marc Behm, Margo Bird, Tony Bramwell, Prudence Bruns, Iris Caldwell, Pattie Clapton, Allan Clarke, Maureen Cleave, Melanie Coe, Richard A Cooke, Nancy Cooke de Herrera, Meta Davis, Rod Davis, Pat Dawson, Richard DiLello, Royston Ellis, Peter Fonda, Johnny Guitar, Paul Horn, Kevin Howlett, Michael Hurll, Stephen James, Rod Jones, Tony King, Timothy Leary, Donovan Leitch, Julian Lennon, Dick Lester, John Duff Lowe, Angie McCartney, Roger McGough, Thelma McGough, Elliot Mintz, Rod Murray, Delbert McClinton, Denis O'Dell, Lucy O'Donnell, Alun Owen, Little Richard, Jimmy Savile, John Sebastian, Helen Shapiro, Don Short, Joel Schumacher, Lucrezia Scott, Derek Taylor, James Taylor, Doug Trendle, Dr John Turner, Jan Vaughan and Gordon Waller.

I also drew on past interviews conducted with Lionel Bart, Hunter Davies, John Dunbar, Cynthia Lennon, George Martin, Barry Miles, Spike Milligan, Roy Orbison, Ravi Shankar, Bruce Welch and Muriel Young.

For supplying information or setting up interviews I thank: Tony Barrow, Penny Bell, Gloria Boyce, Eleanor Bron, Lynne DeBernardis, Liz Edwards, Mike Evans, Peggy Ferguson, Roberta Freymann, Sarah Jane Freymann, Lynda Gilbert, Matt Godwin, Adrian Henri, Corinna Honan, Shelagh Jones, Andrew King, Martha Knight, Carol Lawrence, Mark Lewisohn, Brian Patten, Mrs Juan Mascaró, Robby Montgomery, Peter Nash, Iona Opie, Peter Rhone, Bettina Rose, Juliet Rowe, Phil Spangenberger, Alvin Stardust, Jean Stein, Sue Turner, Lisa Ullmann, Linda Watts and Paul Wayne.

I used facilities supplied by the following organizations: American Federation of Musicians, ASCAP, BMI, Beatles Shop (Liverpool), Bristol Library, Bristol Old Vic, British Library, Chiswick Library, Highland Bookshop and Wildlife Art Gallery (Traverse City, Michigan), National Newspaper Library, National Sound Archives, Nigerian High Commission, Performing Rights Society, Rochdale Library, Theatre Museum, UCLA Library and Westminster Library.

Finally, I would like to thank my agent Lisa Eveleigh who never gave up on the project and Piers Murray-Hill and Jonathan Goodman at Carlton Books.